The ego-"I"
is the Illusion
of Relatedness

The Divine World-Teacher and True Heart-Master,
DA AVABHASA
(The "Bright")

The ego-"I" is the Illusion of Relatedness

The Principal Essay of
The Da Avabhasa Upanishad
by The Divine World-Teacher and True Heart-Master,

Da Avabhasa
(The "Bright")

THE DAWN HORSE PRESS
CLEARLAKE, CALIFORNIA

NOTE TO THE READER

The devotional, Spiritual, functional, practical, relational, cultural, and formal community practices and disciplines discussed in this book, including the meditative practices, the Yogic exercises of "conductivity", the breathing exercises, the life-disciplines of right diet and exercise, the intelligent economization and practice of sexuality, etc., are appropriate and natural practices that are voluntarily and progressively adopted by each student-novice and member of The Free Daist Communion and adapted to his or her personal circumstance. Although anyone may find them useful and beneficial, they are not presented as advice or recommendations to the general reader or to anyone who is not a participant in Da Avabhasa International or a member of The Free Daist Communion. And nothing in this book is intended as a diagnosis, prescription, or recommended treatment or cure for any specific "problem", whether medical, emotional, psychological, social, or Spiritual. One should apply a particular program of treatment, prevention, cure, or general health only in consultation with a licensed physician or other qualified professional.

For a further discussion of individual responsibility in the Way of the Heart, our claim to perpetual copyright to the Wisdom-Teaching of Da Avabhasa, and Da Avabhasa and His Spiritual Instruments and Agents, His renunciate status in The Free Daist Communion, and the Guru-devotee relationship in the Way of the Heart, please see "Further Notes to the Reader", pages 189-91 of this book.

First edition, June 1991
Printed in the United States of America

International Standard Book Number: 0-918801-32-X
Library of Congress Catalog Card Number: 91-073338

Produced by The Free Daist Communion
in cooperation with The Dawn Horse Press

DEDICATION

Heart-Master, Sri Da Avabhasa,

in this book You have Distilled

the essence of Your Wisdom

and Your Promise to Liberate

everyone who responds

as Your true devotee.

May all beings thrill

to the Knowledge that You Are here,

and may everyone be established,

by Your Grace, in the Place

Where You Stand in every heart,

our own and Only Self,

Prior to the illusion of relatedness!

Your devotees

Contents

TO THE READER

Sri Da Avabhasa has developed His own standards and conventions of capitalization (as well as conventions of lowercasing). His purpose has been to create a sacred version of the otherwise worldly, secular, or ego-based English language. His particular usage of capital and lowercase letters is designed, He says, to "interrupt the common flow of mind and Signal your Heart that it is time to Awaken, As You Are."

Out of our respect, gratitude, and love for Heart-Master Da Avabhasa, His devotees capitalize references to Him and His Work and the Heart-Awakeness He Transmits. This is a way for us to acknowledge and indicate to others the Miracle that we find Sri Da Avabhasa to be in our lives. It is also our custom, as it has been of devotees of great Adepts for millennia, to frequently adorn references to our Beloved Guru with honorific praise, as expressions of our acknowledgement of His Divine Nature and Function as Awakener.

Foreword

by Gene R. Thursby

Professor of Religious Studies, University of Florida
author, *Hindu-Muslim Relations in British India*

I am honored to have been asked to contribute a brief statement of appreciation for Sri Da Avabhasa's *The ego-"I" is the Illusion of Relatedness*. In this book, a remarkable Adept displays the revolutionizing wisdom that makes him justifiably known to the world as a "Heart-Master" who awakens others.

With a masterful skill that is engaging from the beginning and then becomes more and more deeply appealing, Sri Da Avabhasa demonstrates how a whole range of traditional formulations of esoteric wisdom are both recapitulated and transcended in what He calls His "Way of the Heart". He reveals their inner logic and the meaningful pattern they form when they come to be understood as components of what He calls the Great Tradition of spiritual teaching.

Although not myself a devotee of Sri Da Avabhasa, I readily acknowledge His singular accomplishment in so clearly expressing this insight into the spiritual nature of reality and so effectively developing it to serve as the basis for a complete way of life. This is a framework for a vital, living, transforming practice that anyone can undertake. And if you become truly serious about it, you will be enabled to grow Spiritually to your utmost capacity within this lifetime. This point is made clearly in a testimony that opens the book, "The Key to This Turnabout", by one of Sri Da Avabhasa's most advanced devotees, Kanya Samatva Suprithi. What she professes and He proclaims is that the one great Accomplishing Principle at the very center of His Way of the Heart is none other than the person and the reality of the Heart-Master, Sri Da Avabhasa Himself.

In the ancient Siddha tradition—and in Zen Buddhism, Hasidic Judaism, Sufi Islam, Eastern and Western mystical Christianity, and other authentic spiritualities that participate in the timeless wisdom of the Great Tradition—the most subtle and profound transmission takes place in the direct contact between the devotee and the Adept. The remarkable book that follows here is an invitation to such a meeting. This is reason enough for it to be regarded as scripture. Weigh its words carefully, and be open to the possibility that Da Avabhasa's presence beyond the words will inspire you to choose a direct and transformative relationship to Him. Because of this book, you may be moved to change your whole way of life.

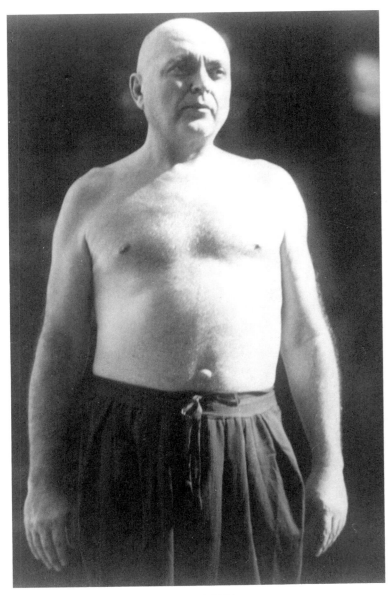

DA AVABHASA
Sri Love-Anandashram

The Way of Transcendence through (and beyond) Relatedness

May All Beings Run to the Person of Truth, Da Avabhasa (The "Bright")!

by Saniel Bonder

It is my deep pleasure, as a devotee of The Divine World-Teacher and True Heart-Master, Da Avabhasa (The "Bright"), to introduce you to His remarkable Essay, "The ego-'I' is the Illusion of Relatedness".

I remember when I first heard about Sri Da Avabhasa, in the summer of 1972. It was through an advertisement for His first book, *The Knee of Listening,* that His devotees had placed in an American magazine. Included in the ad was a quotation from Him that I found extremely intriguing: "Ego is not an entity,

---

TO THE READER: If you are a new reader of Sri Da Avabhasa's literature, you will notice that His use of language is in many ways unique. He has had to develop His own characteristic sacred language in order to describe the Way of the Heart, which is a unique Revelation. In addition to His newly-created Words and Expressions, you will also find traditional Spiritual terms that may have somewhat different meanings here from their traditional usage. We encourage you to familiarize yourself with Sri Da Avabhasa's sacred language by studying the section "A Guide to the Sacred Esoteric Language of the Way of the Heart" and by consulting it frequently as you read.

but an activity." I wondered what He meant by that. Isn't it obvious, I thought, that we are entities, selves, beings? What was the significance of His statement? What were its implications?

These questions meant a lot to me because I had been a relatively frenzied seeker for a few years. I was constantly trying to reach some kind of Spiritual understanding of the ego that would release me from my obvious suffering.

For some time I had been aware of a fundamental dilemma in my comprehension of sacred life and its purposes. Most of my study of Western religion, philosophy, and psychology, and even my childhood upbringing, confirmed in me a feeling that a transformation of relationship is necessary as the key to Spiritual life. Relationship to God, relationship to other human beings, relationship to the world, to life, to my body and mind—the perfect consecration and fulfillment of these as God's gift—this seemed to be the primary category of sacred practice.

But in certain Western Teachings, and in practically all of the Eastern traditions I became aware of, a very different guiding principle stood out: "transcendence". Whatever accommodations were being made to the working out of ordinary and sacred relationships, the whole point of the classically Oriental approaches was to find the best way to "transcend" all relationships, both natural and human, in Divine Oneness with the Ultimate Reality. My study revealed that, in these traditions, the generally recommended means to such "transcendence" was a process of inversion, or even regression from identification with and full participation in the play of life.

I could feel the constant tug in my own being between these two poles of fulfillment and escape, and I did not know what to do about it. In 1972, when I first heard of Sri Da Avabhasa, I was very deeply involved in an extremely inward-turning Oriental meditation practice, looking to be free of the whole miasma of "relationship" and its inevitable difficulties. But at the same time, what to do about love? family? sex?

14

career? ordinary human friendship? I did not know how to answer any such questions.

About a year later, however, I was desperate. The technique of Eastern inwardness I had been engaging had proved itself futile, at a fundamental level. I was still unhappy. I did not know what to do. I longed for relationships to work out, and I also longed for the capability to just bypass or "rise above" the entire ordeal of life and relatedness. It was at this point that I actually came across Da Avabhasa's then published literature. I devoured it.

Almost instantly I felt certain in my heart of two things: first, that this extraordinary Being was and Is absolutely Enlightened and Free; and second, that He was, and Is, my own destined Spiritual Master. And I came upon another of His enigmatic phrases, this one in the form of a Question for use in meditation and at random in daily life: "Avoiding relationship?"

When I first came across Heart-Master Da's Wisdom-Teaching on this practice of what He Calls "self-Enquiry", I had spent several years somewhat desperately turning within. So, for a few pages there, as I read, I wondered if perhaps Da Avabhasa might be Calling His devotees to ask themselves this question— "Avoiding relationship?"—just to make sure that that was, in fact, precisely what they were doing in every moment of life and meditation. I thought the question was, in effect, a recommendation, and it was supposed to have a positive answer: "Yes! I am avoiding relationship—and here's how."

But the more I studied and learned about Sri Da Avabhasa's Wisdom on the nature and activity of the ego, and on His relationship to the actual (and very ordinary and practical) needs of the Westerners who were coming to Him as His first devotees, the more obvious it became that He was Saying something very different from what I first thought. He was pointing to the avoidance of relationship as the activity that is the ego. He was not in any way justifying that activity as an appropriate Spiritual disposition toward life. He was fiercely criticizing such avoidance! But neither was He suggesting some perfection of the ego based on the effort to eliminate the avoidance of relationship.

This was the essence of His Argument: The avoidance of relationship is the ego! By the time I finished reading His second book, *The Method of the Siddhas,* it was quite clear to me that Sri Da Avabhasa intended that His devotees, through their meditative self-Enquiry, see just exactly how, in every moment and at every level of life and mind, they are in fact chronically avoiding relationship and, by that very act, dramatizing egoity.

At the same time, however—and here is the paradox that is pointed to in the title of this present book—by Calling them to understand and transcend the chronic activity of the ego, Sri Da Avabhasa was Calling His devotees to Realize the ultimate Truth that not only transcends every kind and level of the avoidance of relationship, but that really, effectively transcends even all forms of relationship, or relatedness! In other words, in the transcendence of egoity, as Sri Da Avabhasa both Describes and Most Perfectly Demonstrates, the stress of seeking to avoid or attain in the context of relatedness is undone. And even beyond that, the very root presumption that creates the illusory sense of an ego-"I" or relatedness, and the consequent sense of difference and separateness (that we are then driven to overcome), is undone. It is understood and then realized that our natural state is "pleasurable oneness with whatever and all that presently arises" (Da Avabhasa, *The Love-Ananda Gita*).

Let me explain my own mistake a little further, because I feel this discussion may contribute to our right understanding of Sri Da Avabhasa's Instruction in this book and throughout His Way of the Heart. I was, you see, an unwitting perpetrator of one of the most endemic errors of modern Spiritual practitioners—the error that Sri Da Avabhasa sometimes criticizes as the "talking school" approach to ultimate Spiritual Wisdom and Enlightenment.

The ancient, mostly Oriental, Spiritual approaches I was attracted to tended invariably to turn people away from life and relationship. They did so generally on the basis of a philosophical justification that, in the ultimate Realization, "we are all One" or "That thou art"—i.e., the One Transcendental Consciousness that is the Truth is our inherent Nature and therefore we need not bother with the relative, and relatively messy or complicated, dimensions of ordinary, practical life as egos or separate individuals related to others, the world, and a presumed Great Other that is God. We should just affirm and strive to Realize ultimate Truths of Divine Oneness and Consciousness and take our attention off the relativities and dualities of ordinary life and destiny in relationship. After all, those traditional philosophies all seemed to indicate that the world, and all "others" (both limited and Great) are only illusions anyway, concepts within the One Mind.

In my study of Sri Da Avabhasa's Works, it was immediately apparent that His great non-dualistic Affirmations of the essential Oneness of the Divine Reality were based on the most profound Insight into the nature of the ego, and the most profound Realization of the Living Truth of this Inherent Oneness. His Proclamations of this Most Perfect Realization, while foreshadowed by a few rare and supreme Scriptures of Hinduism and Buddhism, were entirely free of the common traditional admonition to disregard manifest existence as an illusion, which admonition stems, really, from the view that life and the complexities of relationship are an irreducible problem.

Sri Da Avabhasa does not acknowledge any legitimacy to proclamations about the nature of the Divine Reality when made by those who have not actually Realized what they proclaim. In later years He spoke specifically of this as a "talking school" error, confusing conceptual thought and speech about ultimate matters of Oneness with the actual, totally body-, emotion-, and mind-transforming discipline that steadies one to receive the Transmission of the Realization of Oneness for real. And that Transmission, Given by Grace of One already fully Realized, is the essential Gift that brings about understanding, transcendence, and Divine Self-Realization Itself.

Because of this, Sri Da Avabhasa took (and certainly takes

in this book) a very active and energetic stance in relation to the apparent dualities and complications of life, mind, and relationship that seemed to bedevil His devotees. He never for a second suggested that anyone just "drop out" and forget about his or her ordinary life—the problems, concerns, and obsessions in the gross areas of "money, food, and sex". Rather, He spelled out increasingly detailed disciplines that His devotees should observe in all such areas, in order—by purifying, strengthening, and energizing their bodies, minds, and hearts—to magnify the process of self-understanding that is central to His Wisdom-Teaching.

Nor did Sri Da Avabhasa merely accept the mystical phenomena that His devotees often spontaneously experience in His Company as sufficient indicators of their Spiritual maturity or Realization of That Which transcends all. Where were the signs in life and in relationship of a truly transformed human character? How thorough and stable are that individual's foundation, in the ordinary dimensions of life and consciousness, for these subtle and ultimate states and capabilities? Were such individuals truly Awake, really transcending body, mind, world, and all relatedness in Conscious Identification with the One Supreme Self? Or were they just "jazzing" themselves with their own interiorized energies, or the "hit" of internal stimulation they could get from His own Potent and tangible Spiritual Presence? Were they therefore, in fact, not only failing to demonstrate mastery of the physical, emotional, mental, and relational foundations of true Spiritual life, but actively refusing to acknowledge even their need for such foundation disciplines and transformations?

Over the course of nearly two decades Sri Da Avabhasa has performed His Liberating Work in ways that clarify, for all future Spiritual aspirants, the course of human and Spiritual preparation that is absolutely necessary for anyone who would Realize the Truth. Yes, He has always Acknowledged, ultimately we Realize the State that is beyond all duality, all relations and relatedness, all sense of a separate "I" over against any kind of "other". But in order to enter into that Realization, we cannot avoid relationship.

In fact the opposite is the case. We must embrace relationship in all forms—human, natural, and Divine—while simultaneously rooting ourselves in the intuition of That Which transcends the "I"-other dualism and is always Free.

How can we possibly do such a thing? Only by entering into a most paradoxical kind of relationship—a relationship to One Who has already Realized the ultimate Truth not only of His own existence but of ours as well. Only such a Person can draw us, via relationship, into the Transcendental Condition beyond and prior to relationship. Sri Da Avabhasa is Himself just such a Person, a Divine Sat-Guru or Revealer of the One Truth.

And what He has done in this short book is provide a crystalline epitome of the entire esoteric Process of Divine Awakening, from its most ordinary and gross beginnings to the most profound developments of Divine Enlightenment. That is part of what makes this book unique. It is a grand overview of the total Process that He Offers, which He expounds in more comprehensive or focused detail in His other Source-Texts: *The Love-Ananda Gita, The Dawn Horse Testament, The Lion Sutra, The Liberator (Eleutherios), The Hymn Of The True Heart-Master, The Basket of Tolerance,* and the greater Text from which this book is drawn, *The Da Avabhasa Upanishad.*

What He is Saying here is also unique, to my knowledge, among any of the traditional texts, Eastern or Western, that address the Great Matter of Divine Enlightenment. This is because no such texts address the total spectrum of this Matter "from the ground up", as Sri Da Avabhasa once said—yet in a way that establishes the whole Process in direct intuition of inherent Freedom. There are many traditional ways of relating to "money, food, and sex". There are many traditional Teachings on ultimate Enlightenment. But this book—*The ego-"I" is the Illusion of Relatedness*—takes each reader through a complete tour of the total Process. And, in it, Sri Da Avabhasa makes it eminently clear how this Way of the Heart is inherently or "always already" founded in the absolute Truth. Through sacred relationship or Communion with Him, in His bodily

Person, Sri Da Avabhasa's devotees enjoy Communion with the Spiritual Presence and the Divine State that transcend all relations even while they intelligently embrace and bring life to all their relations through love.

This is a technically detailed Essay, but its basic structure and flow of Argumentation and Instruction is very simple. In the early sections of His Essay, Sri Da Avabhasa lays the groundwork for everything that is to follow. Principally, He makes it clear how the sacred relationship to Him and His transforming and Enlightening Grace is the key to the Way of the Heart, through a process that He Calls "Ishta-Guru-Bhakti Yoga", meaning "The Way of Divine Union or Oneness through Devotion to One's Chosen, God-Realized Spiritual Master". He then describes the whole process of Divine Awakening via this Great Yoga in terms of the seven stages of life, the seven practicing stages of the technically "fully elaborated" approach to the Way of the Heart, and the five traditional "sheaths" or "bodies" of the human individual that are addressed in certain sacred traditions.

In the middle sections of His Essay, Sri Da Avabhasa then takes us on a step-by-step tour of all of the forms of relationship—to Him, to the world, to others, to our own bodies, minds, and hearts—that we must embrace and master, with His Helping Grace, in order to establish the foundation that allows His Grace to manifest as full Realization of the State that transcends all relatedness. The first and most important work, the foundation, is taking devotional responsibility for the "food body" or physical dimension of our lives, and Sri Da Avabhasa devotes separate sections to extremely detailed Instructions on practice relative to food and sexuality. Always He founds His Recommendations on an ultimate rationale:

Ultimately, What Is Realized Is Self-Sufficient Love-Bliss, or Inherent Happiness, Expressed as Real Freedom and Love (or the "equal eye" of Blessing) toward all beings. Therefore, in order to honor and serve this Realization, all aspects of "money, food, and sex" should be intelligently, progressively, and motivelessly conserved and minimized. Such is the orientation of the practical discipline of the body-mind in the Way of the Heart.

Sri Da Avabhasa then describes, progressively, how the "energy body" and the various levels or dimensions of mind and psyche may be likewise disciplined and aligned to Truth through the devotee's devotion to Him. In these sections of His Essay Sri Da Avabhasa Expounds the process whereby individuals may (if it is necessary for them personally) become proficient in the "ascending" aspect of the Way of the Heart.

This process corresponds to traditional Yogas of ascent of attention through sensitivity to the rising Current of Spiritual Force. Sri Da Avabhasa makes it clear that this process is only necessary for certain of His devotees who have strong karmas in the subtle dimensions of experience and knowledge, and even then only until they can transcend concentration in these dimensions—for these aspects of our possible awareness are just as much to be "intelligently, progressively, and motivelessly conserved and minimized" as our involvement with "money, food, and sex".

In the final sections of His Essay, the Divine Heart-Master Da Gives extensive presentations on His key theme in this book, the transcendence of egoity as the illusion of relatedness. These final sections of the text are among His most poetic and utterly lucid songs of the Contemplation and, ultimately, the continuous Realization of Absolute Divine Consciousness, Transcending all dualities, all bodies, all "sheaths", all relations, all confinement to the illusion of identification with conditional events and phenomena of any kind. Having completely expounded all of the necessary steps that make possible true Freedom from the illusion of relatedness and then Most Perfect Divine Self-Realization, Sri Da Avabhasa now clarifies again and again, and with sublime clarity of expression, how even ordinary people who mature as His devotees may indeed become such Realizers of the Truth.

Most of us suffer a clench of the ego that is so constricting that we spend most of our lives insensitive to the Spiritual Reality. The first effect Sri Da Avabhasa's Grace has on those who practice in His Company is to expose this clench so that, through a most creative and demanding ordeal of self-understanding, we open at heart to receive His Blessing Transmission in Spiritual terms. It is only then, through that hard-won and Grace-Given Spiritual surrender, that we begin to glimpse what He really means by "the feeling of relatedness".

As the practice of the Way of the Heart matures beyond the beginning developmental stages, through Grace-Given transcendence of the self-contraction, we shed the grossest effects of the "avoidance of relationship", and the Bliss of the feeling of no recoil, or the "feeling of relatedness" is uncovered. But as the process continues to deepen, even this Blissful freedom to feel our inherent connectedness or non-problematic relatedness, even continuousness, with all things and beings is gone beyond. The presumption of relatedness, or the feeling of no recoil, at one stage a Blissful revelation, is felt as the root cause or root form of the self-contraction.

The very presumption of being related to an "other" or being an independent or separate "I" in relation to anyone or anything at all, is the fundamental illusion that is the ego. When Sri Da Avabhasa's Blessing Transmission Grants this Understanding and Realization Perfectly, we Stand Free, prior to the self-contraction, as the One Being, Consciousness Itself. The profound Freedom of this "Radical" understanding can only be received through Grace-Given surrender to Sri Da Avabhasa, whereby the gesture of recoil is undone, the feeling of relatedness is felt and transcended, and we are Awakened to stand prior even to this sublime revelation. Such true and "Radical" transcendence is a remarkable ordeal and process.

I would happily give more complete synopses of this process and of each of the sections of this book, but it is not necessary to do so. Readers are very fortunate to have the following testimonial, by one of Sri Da Avabhasa's most mature devotees,

Kanya Samatva Suprithi. Kanya Suprithi provides a compelling account of how she has begun to enjoy the direct Revelation of the Transcendental and inherently Spiritual Truth. She describes with obvious authenticity how she has been Graced by Sri Da Avabhasa to move beyond all compulsive identification with the feeling-illusion of relatedness that is the root of egoity, the core process or activity that tethers or holds in place the egoic, contracted functioning of all the "sheaths" or "bodies" of the body-mind. And her description demonstrates, far better than anything I can say here, the sublime nuances and depths of ultimate practice in the Way of the Heart—the practice for which Sri Da Avabhasa Calls everyone to rapidly prepare in His Company.

The Key to This Turnabout:

An Account of Sri Da Avabhasa's Love-Blissful Feeling of Being and the Way beyond the Illusion of Relatedness

by Kanya Samatva Suprithi

Kanya Samatva Suprithi is a practitioner in the ultimate stages of the Way of the Heart. Formerly Kimberley O'Nan, Kanya Suprithi was born in 1954 in Chicago. She first read Sri Da Avabhasa's books in 1975 and, within weeks, formally became His devotee and a beginning practitioner of the Way of the Heart.

Through her diligent application to Sri Da Avabhasa's Wisdom-Teaching and her reception of His Divine Heart-Blessing, Kanya Suprithi has awakened to a most extraordinary Spiritual and Transcendental Realization. In the following account, she tells how she became first a truly serious practitioner of the Way of the Heart, and then, by Da Avabhasa's Quickening Grace, a practitioner of the "Perfect Practice". Through this ultimate practice in Da Avabhasa's Company, she now consistently and profoundly Stands in the Witness-Position of Free Consciousness and Perfectly transcends the illusion of relatedness. Her Realization—and the simplicity, power, and undeniable authenticity of her confession—make this testimony a most eloquent verification of Sri Da Avabhasa's Revelation. She is a living demonstration of the Great Process of Ishta-Guru-Bhakti Yoga as Expounded by Sri Da Avabhasa in His Essay, "The ego-'I' is the Illusion of Relatedness".

When I first began to practice in Sri Da Avabhasa's Company, it became obvious that, even though I had a strong heart-response to Him, my impulse to God-Realization was weak. My movement to discipline for the sake of Spiritual practice was also weak. I even rebelled against discipline; I disliked it immensely. In fact, that was one of my major difficulties with the practice. But by His Grace and with His Help, I persisted.

Through constantly applying myself to the practice that Sri Gurudev Recommends, by living the disciplines He Recommends, that resistance in me eventually broke down. One of the main things that helped me to overcome that resistance was that I realized that unless I took the disciplines seriously, I was not going to progress in the Way of the Heart.

After thirteen years in Sri Gurudev's Company, I had to face the fact that I was still the same basic character that I was the day I had arrived. I had not really changed. True, I had been Given many Spiritual experiences. I was a more balanced, healthy, happy, and communicative character, but I knew that I was not awakening Spiritually. My point of view, my consciousness, my resistance to discipline fundamentally had not changed, and that was very disturbing to me.

I knew that this was not Sri Gurudev's fault. It was my own doing. I knew that one of the major reasons I had not grown was that I was not applying the discipline fiercely enough. I applied it some times and then did not apply it at other times. In other words, I was not applying it moment by moment and, therefore, I never grew.

The other thing I had not consistently done was to approach Sri Gurudev with total respect and acknowledgement and appreciation for Who He Is as Sat-Guru. In other words, I was not using Him properly. I was still in a very basic sense relating to Him as though He were an ordinary man, which He absolutely is not.

I had not yet accepted the fundamental discipline of surrender to Sri Gurudev as the Divine Person. This is the discipline of Ishta-Guru-Bhakti Yoga—constant self-sacrifice, constant attention to the Sat-Guru's Word, His Requirements, His Demand, the fulfillment of all that He Requires practitioners to fulfill, obedience (or sympathetic conformity to Him), and surrender of the motive in myself to be independent, egoic, willful, self-fulfilling. Without this surrender in relationship to my Sat-Guru, I could not and did not grow. As soon as I did embrace this fundamental discipline of Sat-Guru-devotion, and all the other disciplines that are an expression of that, my growth was amazingly rapid.

This is worth mentioning, because this book communicates about these disciplines, and it outlines them perfectly. My own testimony is that if I had not begun to live the discipline exactly as Sri Gurudev recommends, which is what He is describing in this book, none of the Great Gifts of Awakening and Realization I have since received would have been possible. This is literally true.

It was only after I went through the crisis of accepting the discipline, based on real self-understanding and awakened sensitivity to Sri Da Avabhasa's Spiritual and Always Blessing Presence, that I began to grow in real Spiritual terms. Then I understood what the feeling of relatedness is, and how it is an illusion. Before I made this discovery, which came only after significant Spiritual Gifts were Given to me, I did not even like the concept that the sense of relationship is an illusion. I wondered, "Who doesn't want to be related?" I was not even interested in a Way that was not about relationship.

But now I understand completely what Sri Gurudev means when He speaks of the "illusion of relatedness" and what profound Freedom there is in that understanding. As my practice progressed, I could actually feel the feeling of relatedness as the essence of my self-sense, the essence of the self-contraction. I could feel the sense that everything I perceived was assumed to be related to that. But that very essence or sense of separate self was itself an illusion, and so was the feeling that anything or everything could be related to it.

There was one particular moment in which I was initiated into this understanding by Sri Gurudev. Shortly after I took on the disciplines for real, my practice began to change. Meditation was increased, as were quietude, solitude, and study of Sri Gurudev's Wisdom-Teaching.

In meditation, I began to experience long periods of sublime absorption, feeling absorbed beyond body and mind in Sri Gurudev's Spirit-Presence. I would sit down for a little while, practice the "conductivity" exercises Given for my level of practice at that time. I also practiced self-Enquiry, which would lead to release of the self-contraction in mind and body. In other words, I would stop thinking. No more annoying internal chatter. The body became so profoundly relaxed that it felt very distant, superficial, and I felt as though I were floating or swooning in bliss. I would gradually become more and more absorbed in the Spirit-Current. After a time, I became so deeply absorbed there was no vision, or thought, or bodily motion—just the feeling of Love-Bliss. Just the feeling of falling into that Love-Bliss—for the whole period of meditation, or two hours at each sitting. This began to happen every day, every morning and then again at the night.

I felt so absorbed that I had the feeling that if I just did this enough, I would never come out of that state. I felt it would be as if I walked through a wall and I would not be able to come back. In other words, it would be irreversible. I wanted to stay in that Love-Bliss all the time. I always wanted to feel that way. I felt that this must be Sri Gurudev's State, the Source of His bodily (human) Form and the Consciousness to Which His Spirit-Presence leads. I thought that I had become established in the Witness-Position of Consciousness, just as Sri Gurudev describes in His Wisdom-Teaching. But I was wrong. In fact, I was indulging in a classic traditional error.

During this time, I wrote a summary of my practice and a confession of what was occurring daily in my life and meditation, and offered it to Sri Da Avabhasa for His Blessing. I confessed to Him the profound absorption I felt, and I confessed this absorption was overwhelming, and that I was driven, through my own desire to yield, into this meditative absorption for hours at a time. Never had I felt more intimate with Sri Da Avabhasa. Never had I felt more Love-Bliss than in this meditation. I felt that this must be the right thing to do, and I felt that if I did this a lot, and this absorption became my entire life and consciousness, I would, in essence, be identified with the very same Blissful State and Perfect Oneness I saw so obviously in the Form of my Beloved Sat-Guru, Sri Da Avabhasa.

Sri Gurudev responded swiftly and most directly. After receiving my confession, Sri Da Avabhasa Revealed to me my error in practice. His Response changed my life and practice forever.

Sri Da Avabhasa Said:

> *The Witness-Position of Consciousness is Realized when the search to become absorbed is released and relaxed. No absorption is needed or required for the Realization of the Witness-Position of Consciousness. When the search relative to the first five stages of life relaxes, one realizes that one already stands in the Witness-Position, and that Realization is the basis for the "Perfect Practice".*

Sri Da Avabhasa reminded me again of the "Radical" nature of His Wisdom-Teaching in every stage or level of practice. I saw I was making a profound error, which was seeking experience, seeking absorption, and not transcending experience itself. This Wisdom left me dumbfounded when I went to meditate again.

I had taken the Spiritual search this far, just as they do traditionally, to total absorption in the Guru's Spiritual Presence. When Sri Gurudev Revealed to me that this was not "it", and that this was only more seeking, I felt as though the rug had been taken out from under my feet. I wondered, "If that is not it, then what is it? What do I do now?" I could not go back to the meditation hall and do the same thing, but I did not know what else to do.

When I returned to meditation, I simply sat and began to feel what Is. Instead of seeking the absorptive experience, I now had free energy and attention to feel what was there before this seeking for experience. I desperately resorted to feeling-Contemplation of Sri Da Avabhasa as the only means to move me beyond my habitual tendency to turn everything into my own egoic adventure.

My faith in Sri Da Avabhasa's very bodily (human) Form and Spiritual (and Always Blessing) Presence became my strength. I knew that He alone was sufficient Means for Perfect Realization. I simply resorted to Sri Gurudev. Gradually, I relaxed into observing the forms of self-contraction, rather than continuing the whole process of seeking for experiences. I found that I naturally began to observe forms, conditions, thoughts, and processes, including the process of absorption, rather than yielding to the content of my experience. Soon, I became aware of the essence from which these forms, conditions, thoughts were arising—which is also the root of my seeking for experience. It was the feeling of relatedness itself, which I felt to be at a point in the right side of the heart. It was the root or origin of my own self-identification and the essence of my sense of being differentiated from or in relationship to everything else.

In other words, when I realized that I was really just seeking, I had to resort to Sri Gurudev profoundly to find out how to go beyond this error. I allowed myself to feel Him, rather than merely to experience. And that was the key to the turnabout—feeling Sri Gurudev (As He Is) and using self-Enquiry to transcend the self-contraction. Then I began to feel what Is, prior to experience. The more that I observed things from this stance, the more I began to observe the essence or origin of thoughts, motions, desires, attention itself. That was the beginning of gradually coming to a point where I could locate the feeling of relatedness, as the self-contraction.

Soon, by Grace, I began to feel something very different— the One Feeling or Being That is the Truth, even prior to the feeling of relatedness. The more sympathetic I was with That

One, Who Is Love-Ananda, the more I began to identify with That One. In meditation, I would relax and give myself to That Being. I found that I began to observe thoughts and feelings, experiences, and everything from a stance of sympathy and identification with this Being, prior to the self-contraction.

I saw that I stand as That One, rather than as the mind and thought and the bodily self-sense. I saw that I am, in Truth, the Consciousness that Witnesses all that arises in body and mind and that even Witnesses but always transcends the root essence of egoity, or the feeling of relatedness itself. I also became aware that the Spirit-Current is static, not moving in the body-mind as I had experienced It before, but blissfully resolved in and prior to the right side of the heart. This was very, very deep meditation.

I realized that this root essence (or the feeling of related-ness) was the cause of my sense of separate self, and it was ris-ing from this point in the right side of the heart. It was the sense of "difference", the very sense you have of being related to a something or a someone, to yourself, to an object, to a form, to experience, to any state whatsoever, even to the Spirit-Current. It was paradoxically the first gesture and yet the last remains of this self-sense.

Then I understood Sri Gurudev's admonition that the ego-"I" is the feeling of relatedness. That is exactly what it is. That is exactly what I felt. It was the very essence or point at which I was identified with a separate self, the very origin of that pre-sumption or self-contraction. And it is right there, in the act or sense of being related to objects, forms, thoughts. So now, by Grace, I began to realize that I am not related, I am not a one who can be differentiated or related. And that is mad! It is a total letting go! I am not related. You are not related! You are not an "I", who is related.

Through using Sri Da Avabhasa's "Radical" Words to me and by Contemplating Him most profoundly, I continued to transcend the self-contraction at its root. By His Supreme Grace, He drew me beyond the feeling of relatedness. I found

I could deeply feel the Love-Blissful Feeling of Being, which was always present just prior to the feeling of relatedness. This Love-Blissful Feeling Is Sri Da Avabhasa Himself. This Feeling of Being is Him, and it is also the same as God, Truth, Reality.

It was then that I realized Sri Da Avabhasa to be "Atma-Murti", or the Source of Happiness. I found I was no longer bound to seeking union with or absorption in the Divine. Rather, I discovered the Truth in what Sri Da Avabhasa has always Said. I already inhere in the Divine, or Consciousness Itself, free of the effort to seek union, absorption, or any kind of experience at all. I realized this Happiness was my own State, and this State, or Feeling of Merely Being, was Sri Da Avabhasa Himself. Sri Da Avabhasa was, in fact, and had always been, the Divine State of Merely Being. He is the very Source of this Being Itself. And it is only His Grace that makes this Realization possible.

Sri Da Avabhasa Guided me perfectly, and then so easily Revealed to me the Truth of Himself and also the Truth of myself and everyone. Sri Da Avabhasa is that very Source-Condition. Without this living connection to Sri Da Avabhasa, I would never have found the Way. Without the sheer Attractiveness of Sri Da Avabhasa, I could not have remained interested or impulsed enough to transcend the tendencies and the movement in myself that are bound to the self-contraction and self-despair. Without His exceptional Wisdom, I would never have been drawn beyond the traditional forms of seeking to real Freedom from the illusion of relatedness.

Sri Da Avabhasa Gives everything that His devotee requires. He has Given me everything. It is absolutely true, as they say in the traditions—the Guru is the Means of Spiritual awakening. This is my whole-hearted certainty.

For it is as Sri Da Avabhasa has Said, in His Admonition and Blessing:

By Always Feeling (and, Thereby, Always Contemplating) My Bodily (Human) Form, My Spiritual (and Always Blessing) Presence, and My Very (and Inherently Perfect) State, Always Allow The Divine Person To Stand As all that arises, and (Thus) To Stand Even As Your Own body-mind. If You Truly Do This (With Love, Faith, Devotion, and No Withholding), The Entire Process Associated With Spiritual, Transcendental, and Divine Realization and Liberation Will Be Given To You, Spontaneously, Progressively, and Exactly.

Therefore, Even From The Beginning Of Your Practice Of The Way Of The Heart, Always Feel (and Thereby Contemplate) My Bodily (Human) Form, My Spiritual (and Always Blessing) Presence, and My Very (and Inherently Perfect) State, and Thereby Give Your conditional self (or Release Your self-Contraction) To The Heart-Revealed One, Who Is Always Already Self-Realized (As Consciousness Itself) and Always Already Liberated (or Inherently Free As Love-Bliss Itself).

By This Feeling-Contemplation, The Self-Radiant and Self-Existing Person, Condition, and State Will Be Realized By You, Spontaneously (and Progressively), As A Free Gift.

By This Feeling-Contemplation, You Will See Me Perfectly At Last, As "Atma-Murti" (The "Form" and The "Presence" That Is Inherent Happiness, or Love-Bliss Itself, and The "State" That Is Merely Being, or Consciousness Itself). And You Will Thus (Inherently, Perfectly) Transcend The Illusion Of Separation and Relatedness.

OM SRI DA AVABHASA HRIDAYAM

32

All I can add here is my own acknowledgement that these Words of Sri Da Avabhasa are Full of Awakening Power. Indeed, one or another of the last five sections of this Essay is recited aloud, at His Gracious Recommendation, by His devotees as part of our morning devotions one or more times each week. Anyone who attends to His Discourse here with an open mind and a receptive heart is certain to be deepened in the Wisdom and the actual Intuition of Freedom, Enlightenment, and Happiness, the State that transcends the egoic activity of the illusion of relatedness. But then, to actually Realize that Happy State permanently—there is the whole process that He has Revealed, and none of it can be bypassed; but all of it can be immeasurably Quickened by His Grace.

And the Key to the whole process is that by attending to Sri Da Avabhasa's Words, we are attending to Him, in Person. He is the living Truth of Consciousness, the Divine Person, the Very Self of the world, Alive in a single bodily (human) Form so that all others may Realize our inherent Freedom in Perfect Identification with Him. Because His Wisdom embraces and comprehends all of the previous formulations of understanding that humanity has ventured—as this Essay should make eminently clear to anyone who seriously studies it—and because He actively Embraces and Blesses and, paradoxically, Lives as every single living being through His universal, All-Pervading, Divine Heart-Blessing as the Supreme Self, Sri Da Avabhasa's devotees proclaim Him to all as both The Divine World-Teacher and The True Heart-Master. May all beings run to the Person of Truth, Da Avabhasa (The "Bright")!

S.B.

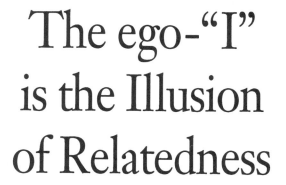

The ego-"I"
is the Illusion
of Relatedness

The Principal Essay from
The Da Avabhasa Upanishad
by The Divine World-Teacher and True Heart-Master,

Da Avabhasa
(The "Bright")

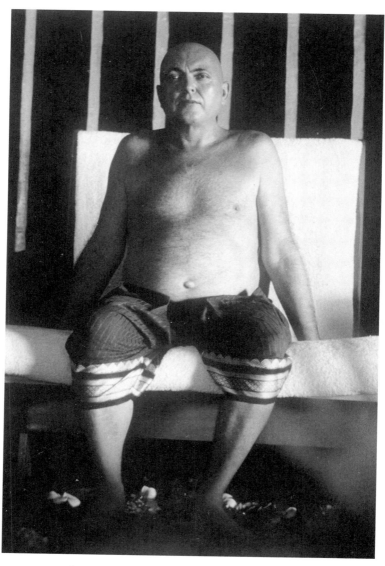

The Divine World-Teacher and True Heart-Master,
DA AVABHASA
(The "Bright")

The ego-"I" is the Illusion of Relatedness

The Divine World-Teacher and True Heart-Master,

Da Avabhasa
(The "Bright")

I

T he total Way that I have Revealed is called "Daist", or, more properly, "Free Daist", the Inherently Free Way that Freely becomes Devotion to, and Communion with, and Realization of the by Grace Revealed Divine Person (and Self-Condition), Who is called "Da" ("The One Who Gives"), and Who <u>Is</u> Freedom (or Always Already Free Being, Love-Bliss-"Brightness", and Consciousness Itself), and Who is Revealed by and <u>As</u> the bodily (human) Form, the Spiritual (and Always Blessing) Presence, and the Very (and Inherently Perfect) State of the Hridaya-Samartha Sat-Guru (or Adept Heart-Teacher and True Heart-Master), Who I Am.

The Free Daist Way is most generally called either "The Way of the Heart" (or "The Religion of 'Sri Hridayam'") or "The Way of 'Radical' Understanding". The Free Daist Way is also called "Hridaya Advaitism" (the Heart-Way of Non-Dualism, or of Non-"Different", or Non-Separate, Truth), and "Hridaya-Advaita Dharma" (or the Teaching, the Way, and the Truth of the Non-Dual, and Non-"Different", or Non-Separate, Heart), and "Hridaya-Advaita Yoga" (or the Yoga, Way, or Practice of "Hridaya Advaitism"), or, simply, "'Radical' Advaitism" (or the Way of most direct and, ultimately, Inherently Perfect Realization of the One and Non-Separate "Bright" Condition That Is God, Truth, and Reality).[1]

The Free Daist Way is the Heart-Way and the "Radical" Process of most direct (and, ultimately, Inherently Perfect) feeling-Contemplation of the Inherent Reality (or Unconditional Existence) That <u>Is</u> Happiness Itself, and this Heart-Way of "Radical" Practice (and, ultimately, of Non-Dualistic Enlightenment) Realizes (ultimately, and by Grace) the Ultimate Nature (or Perfectly Subjective Source-Condition) That <u>Is</u> Happiness Itself. Therefore, in its total (and, ultimately, Perfect) course, the Free Daist Way both epitomizes and exceeds, or Most Perfectly Fulfills, the universal human aspiration to escape, overcome, or utterly transcend any and every apparent "problem" (even, ultimately, the apparent "problem" that is conditional, or apparently separate and limited, existence itself).

Indeed, the entire Great Tradition of mankind (including all religious and Spiritual traditions, and all traditional Yogas, or even all traditional approaches, and even all possible approaches, to Real Happiness, God-Realization, Ultimate Liberation, and Perfect Freedom) is epitomized and Fulfilled in the Free Yoga (or "Radical" Way of the Heart) that I have Revealed.

---

1. Sri Da Avabhasa occasionally uses traditional Sanskrit terms because of their condensed, and Spiritually evocative, meanings. "Hridaya" means "heart", and refers to Consciousness or Being Itself. "Advaita" means "non-dual". And "Dharma" refers to Sri Da Avabhasa's Wisdom-Teaching, and also to the Practice and Realization of the Way of the Heart in His Company.

The Way of the Heart is the "Radical" (or most direct) Way (or Yoga) of "Satsang" (or the "Good and Persistent Company of Truth"). It is the Practice and the Process of Sat-Guru Satsang (or Sat-Guru-Satsang Yoga, or, simply, Satsang Yoga). Therefore, the Way of the Heart is the Practice and the Process of Persistence in the fullest Devotional (or self-surrendering, self-forgetting, and self-transcending) Resort to Me, the Hridaya-Samartha Sat-Guru, for I Am the Realizer, the Revealer, and the Revelation of Truth (Which Is Self-Existing and Self-Radiant Being, Itself).

The Primary Yoga, or Root-Practice, of the Way of the Heart is Ishta-Guru-Bhakti Yoga, the Yoga of Devotion to Me As the "Chosen One" of one's Heart (and As the Realizer, the Revealer, and the Revelation of the Form, and the Presence, and the State of the Divine Person and Self-Condition). Therefore, the Way of the Heart is (and more and more Fully, and then Perfectly, becomes) the Way of Ishta-Guru-Bhakti Yoga, in which the conditional self (and its world) is (progressively) transcended in the feeling-Contemplation of My bodily (human) Form, My Spiritual (and Always Blessing) Presence, and My Very (and Inherently Perfect) State.

This Way (or Yoga) of the Heart is, in practice, a progressive Process. At first it is associated (but in a uniquely self-transcending manner) with the "great path of return" (or progressive self-transcendence in the context of the first six stages of life). Ultimately, it is established in the Transcendental (and Inherently Spiritual) Divine Yoga of Consciousness Itself, or the seventh stage of life, in which the body-mind and the world are Inherently Outshined (or Dissolved in the Inherent Heart-"Brightness") through Divine Self-Abiding and Inherent (Sahaj, or "Natural", or Divinely Self-Realized) Recognition of all conditions as they arise (in and As the Transcendental and Inherently Spiritual Divine Self, or Self-Existing and Self-Radiant Consciousness Itself).

II

All the forms of the by Me Revealed and Given Way of the Heart, and all the moments and degrees of Realization in the technically "simpler" (or even "simplest") form and course of the by Me Revealed and Given Way of the Heart, and all the practicing stages (or all the stages of progressive discipline and Realization) in the technically "fully elaborated" (or "elaborately detailed") form and course of the by Me Revealed and Given Way of the Heart, and even all the progressive disciplines (or Yogas) found in the traditions (or the one and all-encompassing Great Tradition in which the by Me Revealed and Given Way of the Heart has appeared) should be understood in the context of the seven stages of life (and also in the context of the primary structures of the body-mind). All forms, moments, degrees, and developmental stages of the Way of the Heart, and even all progressive Yogas (or all traditional Means or Ways of Realizing present Union or Prior Identification with the Spiritual and Transcendental Divine), involve progressive transcendence of the body-mind (or a "great path of return", through and beyond the structural levels of the body-mind).

This progressive Process is related to the key centers in the body-mind, the principal functions of the body-mind, and the natural Circuit (including the Circle and the Arrow) whereby these centers and functions are projected within and onto Consciousness. Just so, the Process is a step-by-step passage through and beyond the key centers, the principal functions, and the natural Circuit of the body-mind, until Consciousness Itself Realizes Its Inherent Supremacy and Fullness, thus making progressive practice (or the "great path of return" itself) unnecessary.

In the Way of the Heart, which is the Way that I have Completed, Perfected, Revealed, and Given (even by always presently Giving it), this Process is fully understood and embraced as a whole (even stage of life by stage of life). And

40

the technically "fully elaborated" (or "elaborately detailed") course of the Way of the Heart is the form of the Way of the Heart in which practice is most thoroughly developed (or elaborated) in terms of technical stages of practice.

Both the technically "fully elaborated" (or "elaborately detailed") course of the Way of the Heart and the technically "simpler" (or even "simplest") course of the Way of the Heart are built upon the (initial and preparatory) student-novice stage (or the formal, and listening-active, "applicant's stage") of the original approach to the Way of the Heart and the subsequent student-beginner stage (or "foundation stage") of formally acknowledged[2] practice of the Way of the Heart.

The technically "simpler" (or even "simplest") course of the Way of the Heart involves the progressive development of listening (or self-surrendering and self-forgetting Devotional "consideration" relative to the first three stages of life, and in the "original", or beginner's, Devotional context of the fourth stage of life) and true hearing (or most fundamental self-understanding, and the exercise of the thereby Awakened capability for direct self-transcendence) and clear seeing (or Spiritually activated Heart-Practice). And the technically "simpler" (or even "simplest") course of the Way of the Heart develops (potentially, or as necessary) in the context of each and all of the seven stages of life.

The general technical practices associated with the "conscious process" in the technically "simpler" (or even "simplest") course of the Way of the Heart remain basically the same in the context of each and all of the developing stages of life, once that "simpler" (or even "simplest") technical practice of the "conscious process" is established (in the initial, or student-beginner, stage of the Way of the Heart). However, the technical practices associated with the developing practice of

2. The disciplines of the Way of the Heart can be truly effective only when practiced in the context of a direct and formally acknowledged relationship to Sri Da Avabhasa, in which case the practitioner embraces the total discipline of the Way of the Heart and participates as fully as possible in the total culture of other formally acknowledged practitioners.

"conductivity" in the technically "simpler" (or even "simplest") course of the Way of the Heart are, in general, the same practices engaged by practitioners of the technically "fully elaborated" form of the Way of the Heart (and all "conductivity" practices in the Way of the Heart are, in the progressive course of the Way of the Heart, developed from the original "conductivity" practices embraced by even all practitioners of the Way of the Heart in the initial, or student-beginner, stage of the Way of the Heart).

The technically "fully elaborated" (or "elaborately detailed") course of the Way of the Heart involves seven (potential) practicing stages, and these develop in the context of the seven stages of life. However, in the technically "elaborately detailed" course of the Way (or Yoga) of the Heart, the seven stages of life and the seven practicing stages do not correspond to one another numerically (number by number), except in the case of practicing stages five, six, and seven (which correspond to the fifth, sixth, and seventh stages of life respectively). Practicing stages one through four of the technically "fully elaborated" form of the Way of the Heart each correspond to a progressive development of the fourth stage of life (beginning also in the context of the first three stages of life). Indeed, practice of even any by Me Given form of the Way of the Heart is initially a culture of self-transcendence in the general context of the first three stages of life (based in the "original", or beginner's, Devotional context of the fourth stage of life), and then, progressively, toward and to the seventh stage of life, stage by stage (as necessary). And, of course, the "Radical", or Inherently Perfect, Disposition of the seventh stage of life informs and inspires the practice at even every stage of life in the Way of the Heart.

Following the student-novice stage (of formal approach to the Way of the Heart) and the student-beginner stage (of formally acknowledged practice of the Way of the Heart), practicing stage one of the technically "fully elaborated" form of the Way of the Heart continues (and further develops) the process of listening (or self-surrendering and self-forgetting Devotional "consideration") relative to the first three stages of life (in the "original", or beginner's, Devotional context of the fourth stage of life), and (in the form of eventual true hearing, or most fundamental self-understanding) practicing stage one of the technically "fully elaborated" form of the Way of the Heart regenerates the effective capability for direct self-transcendence (which capability progressively releases the body-mind via the Heart-Response that characterizes the fourth stage of life).

Practicing stage two of the technically "fully elaborated" form of the Way of the Heart Awakens clear seeing, or the Devotional and Spiritual Heart-Practice that characterizes the ("basic") Spiritually established fourth stage of life.

Practicing stage three of the technically "fully elaborated" form of the Way of the Heart develops fully responsible practice of all "basic" (or frontal and descending) aspects of the fourth stage of life.

Practicing stage four of the technically "fully elaborated" form of the Way of the Heart is the "advanced" (and ascending, or spinal) stage of the technically "fully elaborated" practice of the Way of the Heart in the context of the fourth stage of life, and it is at (or via) this practicing stage of the technically "fully elaborated" form of the Way of the Heart that the natural (psycho-physical) transition is made from the context of the fourth stage of life to that of the fifth stage of life.

The transition to practicing stage five of the technically "fully elaborated" form of the Way of the Heart is the transition to the technically "fully elaborated" practice of the Way of the Heart in the context of the fifth stage of life, or the Spiritual Process of the ascent of attention via (or through, or from) the Ajna Door (or the brain core, deep behind and between and slightly above the brows), and via (or through, or from) the upper reaches of the subtle mind, to the crown of the head (and beyond, to ascended Realization above and beyond the body, its brain, and the mind).

The transition to practicing stage six of the technically "fully elaborated" form of the Way of the Heart, or to the technically "fully elaborated" practice of the Way of the Heart in the context of the sixth stage of life, is made when the binding motives and errors of practice associated with each and all of the first five stages of life are really transcended and Identification with the Witness-Consciousness is Perfect (or Inherently, effortlessly, and stably the case).

The transition to practicing stage six of the technically "fully elaborated" form of the Way of the Heart will (by Grace) be made (in most cases) directly from practicing stage three of the technically "fully elaborated" form of the Way of the Heart, once clear signs of basic maturity in practicing stage three are demonstrated. Otherwise (in the case of a relative few practitioners of the Way of the Heart, and only because of their unusually strong subtle tendencies of mind), the transition to practicing stage six of the technically "fully elaborated" form of the Way of the Heart will be made either at maturity (if not earlier) in practicing stage four of the technically "fully elaborated" form of the Way of the Heart or at some advanced (or even earlier) moment in practicing stage five of the technically "fully elaborated" form of the Way of the Heart.[3]

The total Process of the Way of the Heart in the context of the first six stages of life (and in the context of the first six practicing stages of the technically "fully elaborated" form of the Way of the Heart) can also be called the Yoga of "Consideration". That Yoga or Way is Full (or Complete) when Sahaj Samadhi (or the Awakening that Initiates and Characterizes the seventh stage of life) is Realized.

Practicing stage seven of the technically "fully elaborated" form of the Way of the Heart (or the Demonstration of the Way of the Heart in the technically "fully elaborated" context of the

3. The entire Way of the Heart is a matter of the transcendence of attention in the Heart, rather than an effort to return to the Heart or Divine Self by an exhaustive process of experience. In the Way of the Heart, no experience is necessary. The progressive practice serves to awaken, strengthen, and stabilize the practitioner's hearing, or most fundamental self-understanding, and seeing, or emotional conversion to and stable Spiritual reception of Sat-Guru Da's Spiritual (and Always Blessing) Presence. When there is basic Spiritual maturity (in the "basic" context of the fourth stage of life in the Way of the Heart), many, or even most, devotees will, through Grace, be drawn into the Witness-Position of Consciousness, which inherently transcends the search for experience that characterizes the first five stages of life. The sixth stage of life begins when we begin to merely observe all phenomena from the Witness-Position of Consciousness.

seventh stage of life) is a spontaneous and progressive Demonstration of the Signs of Divine Transfiguration and Divine Transformation, until the Signs of Divine Indifference spontaneously begin to be Demonstrated.

The Ultimate Demonstration of practicing stage seven of the technically "fully elaborated" form of the Way of the Heart is Divine Translation (the Outshining of conditional existence in the Inherent and Infinite "Bright" Love-Bliss of Divine Self-Existence).

III

The body-mind is progressively transcended by the transcendence of egoity (or self-contraction) in the context of each of the functional levels of the body-mind. This Process moves from the gross functions toward the subtle functions, and from the frontal line (or the frontal personality, or the gross personality) to the spinal line (or the subtle personality), until the Process of the transcendence of the central, or causal, dimension of the apparent or conditional personality (associated with the right side of the heart) becomes the Direct Means for the Realization of Consciousness Itself.

In fact, if the various primary functional levels of the body-mind can be rightly perceived and (most fundamentally) understood, then the key to each developmental stage of practice is Revealed. And this right perception and most fundamental understanding is already suggested by the traditional names for the functional levels (or sheaths, or coverings, or superimpositions on Consciousness) represented by the body-mind:[4]

The gross body, or the physical body, is annamayakosha, the food sheath, or the food body.

___

4. In this Essay, Sri Da Avabhasa describes the human body-mind in terms of the system of five koshas (or sheaths) first described in the *Taittiriya Upanishad*. In contrast to traditional esoteric Spirituality, Heart-Master Da has Revealed that any and all actions that pursue Divine Self-Realization through the manipulation of the koshas are false and ultimately futile.

The subtle body, or the internal personality (or group of functions), is made of three functional parts. The first (which may be contacted inwardly, but which is really surrounding the gross body) is pranamayakosha (the pranic sheath, or the pranic body, or the body of personal life-energy). The second is manomayakosha (or the sheath of lower mind). The lower mind includes the conscious mind, the subconscious mind, and the unconscious mind, and the functional activity of the lower mind (or brain-mind) is generated from a position that stands above and senior to the pranic body. The third (and most senior) part of the subtle body is vijnanamayakosha (the sheath of higher mind, the sheath of superconscious mind, or the sheath of intellect). At the core of the higher mind is the central will and discriminative (and naturally observant) intelligence of the conditional "I", or limited self, and its functional activity is generated from a position that stands above and is central and senior to the sheath of lower mind.

Finally, there is anandamayakosha, the sheath of conditional bliss, or the causal body, which is the causative root of conditional selfhood. The true causal body is associated with the right side of the heart (which is itself the Ultimate Passageway to Transcendental Self-Consciousness).

In some Yogic traditions, the term "subtle body" is used to indicate only pranamayakosha (the pranic body, or the etheric body). Then the term "causal body" is used to indicate only the lower mind (or manomayakosha), and the term "supercausal body", or "supracausal body", is used to indicate the higher or superconscious mind (which is vijnanamayakosha).

In such traditions, Yogic Liberation is usually conceived in terms of the ascent of attention, via the spinal line of the Spirit-Current, penetrating and going beyond all layers of body and mind in its course, until it Merges in the Akasha (or the Infinite Ascended Space) of Spirit-Consciousness, Above the worlds. Some Yogis also associate Final Enlightenment with a subsequent descent of attention from such ascended (and thus conditional, and fifth stage) Nirvikalpa Samadhi to the highest position (or point, or spot of concentration) in the so-called "supra-causal", or superconscious, mind, associated with the central and extreme upper region of the brain. That point or spot is often visualized (as a bindu, or a spot of light), or also heard (as nada-bindu, or a concentrated point of light and sound), or else it may simply be felt (and thus "touched") as a blissful locus (or loka) of the Spirit-Current (or Shakti), without visual or auditory associations. Thereafter, all conditional forms are seen, heard, or felt (via that brain-locus of light, or sound, or touch) as a Play in the Divine Mind.

Such traditions epitomize the fifth stage of life. In that view, the "soul" (which is simply the subtle body, as a whole, or in part) is <u>conditionally</u> Liberated via the ascent of attention, but even in the case of such Yogic Liberation, the "soul" (or the ego, identified as an eternal individual) remains intact (and in conditional, and only temporary, Communion with God).

In the fifth stage tradition of Yogic Liberation (which is to be contrasted with the tradition of Direct, or Transcendental, Liberation, associated with the sixth and seventh stages of life), the sheaths, or koshas, correspond to the sounds and lights (and other subtle perceptions) that are experienced in ascending meditation. The various sounds and lights correspond to the progressive vibratory levels of the Cosmic Mandala (or the Spirit-Current modified as the Sphere, or Circle, or Wheel, of Cosmic Manifestation). Annamayakosha (or the gross body) is seen in the form of a red light (or a range of possible lights, from red through yellow), corresponding to the outer ring (or rings) of the Cosmic Mandala. Pranamayakosha (or the "subtle body" of the fifth stage Yogis) is seen as a pale (or moonlike) white light. Manomayakosha (or the "causal body" of the fifth stage Yogis) is seen as a black light, or dark field. And vijnanamayakosha (or the "supracausal body" of the fifth stage Yogis) is seen as a radiant blue light (the bindu, or what some describe as a "blue pearl"). Likewise, the various sounds perceived in ascending meditation also arise in a hierarchy of progressive subtlety, from grosser (and louder) toward finer (and quieter) sounds.

47

Since vijnanamayakosha is the root-mind, or the "I" of the mind, the fifth stage Yogis say that the vision of the "blue pearl" is the vision of the Transcendental and Divine Self. In Truth, it cannot, as itself, Be the Transcendental Divine Self, since the Transcendental Divine Self Is the Transcendental Divine Subject of phenomena, and, therefore, It Is the Witness of objects, and not Itself an object. The bindu is simply the highest conditional state and form and locus of the subtle body (or that form of the subtle body which the fifth stage Yogis call the "supracausal body"). Therefore, the vision of the bindu (or "blue pearl") is itself the most subtle form (and preoccupation) of the ego, or the mind of the conditional self. This is My experience, and My firm conclusion from experience of these very things.

When vijnanamayakosha is penetrated in (fifth stage) conditional Nirvikalpa Samadhi, the colored lights (or rings) of the Cosmic Mandala (and all sounds and other perceptions otherwise apparent within the experiential, or psycho-physical, context of the Cosmic Mandala) are temporarily penetrated and transcended at their core, and the Brilliant White Five-Pointed Star and the Infinite Clear Space of Brilliant Whiteness (and Vast Silence) at the Center of the Cosmic Mandala are temporarily entered. Even so, the True Transcendental Self (Which Is not phenomenal, or conditional, or experiential, or of the mind, or of the body, or of the egoic self, but Which Is Consciousness Itself) must eventually be Realized. Thus, after some time, the ascent of attention must cease to be a driving impulse. Then attention begins to relax or subside in its Perfectly Subjective Source or Ground (via spontaneous Identification with the Witness-Consciousness), and the Spirit-Current begins to come to rest in Its Ultimate and Perfectly Subjective Source (the Aham Sphurana, or the Love-Bliss-Feeling of Being Itself, associated with the right side of the heart).

This Inherently Perfect Process is the penetration of the final (or root) conditional (and egoic) knot, or body, or sheath, or kosha, which is the true anandamayakosha (the true causal body, associated with the right side of the heart). This penetration Realizes Transcendental Awareness (or Consciousness Itself), and Transcendental Existence (or Inherent and Self-Existing Being) Itself, and Transcendental Love-Bliss (or Inherent and Self-Radiant Happiness) Itself, Inherently and Inherently Perfectly beyond body, emotion, natural life-energy, thought, planes of mind, speech, visions, auditions, tastes, odors, touches, worlds, phenomenal beings, and every form or perception of the Cosmic Mandala of conditional existence. Thus, when anandamayakosha is penetrated and transcended, and all conditions are Divinely Recognizable, Consciousness Itself Abides <u>As</u> Its Own Inherent and Divine Love-Bliss, or Shakti,[5] or Soundless "Sound", or Non-Objective "Light", or Inherently "Bright" Self-Existing Self-Radiance. And, therefore, the Light (or the "Bright") That Is Itself the Divine is not seen as an Object. Transcendental or Very (and necessarily Divine) Consciousness (Self-Existing and Self-Radiant) Shines Only <u>As</u> Itself, not <u>To</u> Itself.

Every object, however Great, is only an apparent Reflection of the Transcendental and Inherently Spiritual Divine Self, like the face of Narcissus (shining in his own pond). The Self-Radiant and Self-Existing Being Is the Ground and Reflecting Screen of Its Own apparent modifications. All objects are only Illusions, or merely apparent modifications of the Self-Existing Divine Self-Radiance. When This Is Realized, the Transcendental and Inherently Spiritual Divine Self Is Awakened from the Illusion of all objects and others, and It Is Self-Released from the fear and the insult of seeming separation from Love-Bliss. Thus Awakened, the Transcendental Divine Self simply Stands As Itself, Shining As Its Own Love-Bliss, Shining through the now transparent (or merely apparent) imagery of body, mind, and worlds, until the "Bright" Inherent Love-Bliss Outshines the seeming "things".

---

5. The Transcendental and Unmodified Divine Shakti should not be confused with any (conditional) natural, etheric, or esoteric energies that are circulated or conducted in the manifest body-mind. The Shakti of which Heart-Master Da Speaks is Hridaya-Shakti, the Moveless Power of the Heart, or Consciousness Itself.

The Way of the Heart is not limited to the purposes and attainments associated with the fifth stage of life. In My view (and experience) all of the conditional, or egoic, bodies (or sheaths) are to be penetrated (or transcended), to the Degree of Divine Enlightenment, or the Awakening (and the Ultimate Process) associated with the seventh stage of life. If this is to be the case, the Preliminary Process (or the Yoga of "Consideration") must continue beyond (and may even bypass) the Yoga of ascending attention (or the fifth stage of life). The Complete Process of the Yoga of "Consideration" requires transcendence of attention itself, in the context of the sixth stage of life (or the Process of the penetration and transcendence of the causal knot, or the original egoic contraction, associated with the right side of the heart).

Therefore, in My "consideration" of the stages of life, I make use of the traditional descriptions of the sheaths, but I find the description of five sheaths to be the most accurate and complete. Thus, there is one gross sheath (and it is primarily associated with the frontal, descended, or descending, personality). There are three subtle sheaths, and they are associated, in their lower range, with the frontal line, or the gross personality, and, in their upper range, with the spinal line, or the subtle personality (whether in the gross or the exclusively subtle context). And there is one causal sheath, originating in association with the right side of the heart. Just so, if these sheaths (or levels) of psycho-physical existence are really and rightly perceived, and (most fundamentally) understood (so that they are Released from the binding and deluding motive of self-contraction), and (most directly) transcended, then passage through and beyond the limits of the first six stages of life can be truly accelerated (and soon, and Inherently, Perfected).

IV

A characteristic of mind, or the structural personality in general, is that it tends to interpret (whatever it perceives) according to its own point of view, or level of vision. Therefore, individuals with a strictly gross level of perception may tend to perceive and interpret the conditional reality as strictly physical (or gross). Those with a more etheric (or lower subtle) point of view may perceive and interpret the conditional reality at a more etheric level. And so on. Such are the limits that the strictly programmed personality creates and projects.

From the beginning of practice in the Way of the Heart, the practitioner of the Way of the Heart is Called to <u>feel</u> (and thereby to Contemplate) My bodily (human) Form, My Spiritual (and Always Blessing) Presence, and My Very (and Inherently Perfect) State, but his or her perception of My bodily (human) Form and My Spiritual (and Always Blessing) Presence, and his or her awareness of My Very (and Inherently Perfect) State, will tend to be limited by his or her perception in mind. Therefore, the essence of the practice is to surrender through a self-transcending gesture of the heart, a gesture that allows for an ever greater, or (progressively) Spiritual, Transcendental, and (ultimately) Divine, perception of My bodily (human) Form and My Spiritual (and Always Blessing) Presence, and awareness of My Very (and Inherently Perfect) State.

When practitioners of the Way of the Heart are Called to feel (and thereby to Contemplate) My bodily (human) Form, and My Spiritual (and Always Blessing) Presence, and My Very (and Inherently Perfect) State, they are Called to heart-surrender, such that the feeling-Contemplative perception of My bodily (human) Form and My Spiritual (and Always Blessing) Presence serves direct feeling-Contemplation of, or intuitive Communion (and, ultimately, Inherent, and Inherently Perfect, Identification) with, My Very State, Which is the Inherently Perfect Samadhi of the Divine Self-Condition.

In that Process, an ever greater perceptual and intuitive capability will (and must) be generated. Thus, for example, all student-beginners in the Way of the Heart, and all practitioners in the intensive listening-hearing stage of the Way of the Heart, and also all children and young people in the Way of the Heart, are Called to develop an awareness of the etheric. Such sensitivity to the etheric dimension of conditional existence is fundamental to what I call "conscious exercise". (Indeed, an awareness of the etheric should be basic to the context of learning for all human beings in the first three stages of life. However, it is obvious that, in a materialistic society, such is not generally part of people's learning. Rather, sensitivity to the etheric is suppressed in favor of a strictly materialistic, or gross physical, awareness.)

Truly Spiritual practice of the Way of the Heart (and, thus, actual Communion with the Love-Bliss-Radiance of the Divine Person and Self-Condition) first develops (by Grace) in the context of the fourth stage of life in the Way of the Heart. Therefore, in the Way of the Heart, Spiritual practice requires the foundation of the beginner's responsive (or Devotional) practice of heart-surrender in all its (by Me Given) forms. Only on the basis of the true and effective completion of the beginner's listening-hearing ordeal of preparation for (full and fullest) Spiritual Communion with Me (and, Thus and Thereby, with the Divine Person and Self-Condition), and (on that continued basis) only in the event of Spirit-Baptism in My Heart-Company (and in the context of the Acknowledgement and Embrace of Me as True Heart-Master), does the practice of the Way of the Heart begin to develop (as a matter of direct and full responsibility) in Spiritual terms.

By "Spiritual" I do not mean merely "subtle", or (in other words) the experience of moving from the gross physical to the etheric (or lower subtle) and then to the middle and higher ranges of the subtle. Experientially, even the beginner in the Way of the Heart may (by Grace) have subtle experiences (and even Spiritual experiences) of one kind or another in the practice of (and in all the practices rightly associated with) feeling-Contemplation of My bodily (human) Form, My Spiritual (and Always Blessing) Presence, and My Very (and Inherently Perfect) State, but the Divine Spirit Itself is not to be identified with any subtle body. In fact, the Divine Spirit infuses (or pervades and inherently transcends) all five of the conditionally manifested bodies (or sheaths).

My Spirit-Baptism is the Transmission of the Inherent Force of the Divine Self. In the context of the bodily-based personality in the first three stages of life, the Divine Spirit is (or may be) felt in gross (physical) and etheric terms (or, simply, as gross and etheric functions and events). Even in the earliest beginnings of practice in the "original" (or foundation) context of the fourth stage of life in the Way of the Heart, when there may be some (beginner's) response to My Spiritual (and Always Blessing) Presence, experiences are generally associated with gross physical and etheric awareness.

As individuals develop more fully in the "basic" Spiritual context of the fourth stage of life in the Way of the Heart, Spiritual awareness develops (and must develop) to a greater degree, and there is (or must be) a greater ability to directly identify the (by Grace Revealed) Spirit-Power (Itself) and to be responsible to surrender the gross physical dimension, and the etheric dimension, and even the mental-psychic (or the middle range of the subtle) dimension of the bodily-based personality into It. This is why I Say that, in the Way of the Heart, the Spiritual Process cannot truly (or responsibly) begin until there is true hearing (or most fundamental, and directly effective, self-understanding) and entrance (by Means of My Spirit-Baptism) into the fully established "basic" (or truly Spiritual) context of the fourth stage of life. Then, if necessary, in the "advanced" (or ascending) context of the fourth stage of life, and in the (possible) fifth stage of life, awareness of the Divine Spirit develops further, in the ascending context of the Way of the Heart, and relative to experiences in the higher range of the subtle dimension.

Even all the experiences and developments in the Circle (and the Arrow) of the body-mind are Spiritual only in the sense, or to the degree, that they are being submitted to (and transcended in) the Divine Spirit. The conditionally manifested bodies (or sheaths, or dimensions) are not themselves Spiritual. In other words, there is nothing inherently Spiritual about the gross physical, or the etheric, or the mental-psychic, or the higher psychic aspects of the personality.

Therefore, in the Way of the Heart, all the conditionally manifested bodies (or sheaths) are to be submitted to the Divine Spirit (and transcended in that submission). In this, the Way of the Heart stands in contrast to many of the world's religious and Spiritual traditions, wherein these bodies (or potentials for experience) are (often) developed for their own sake and presumed to be Spiritual (in themselves), as are their experiences (themselves). On the basis of this (erroneous) view, the development of these bodies (or their conditional experiences) is therefore presumed to be the Spiritual Process Itself.

The Divine Spirit is prior to (and is not to be equated with) the mechanics of conditional Nature, and all its dualities (both yin and yang), and all the bodies (or sheaths) of the conditionally manifested individual. Therefore, yin and yang have nothing directly (in and of themselves) to do with the Spirit-Current (or Divine Shakti). To say that they do is a conventional interpretation made, generally, by people who are not Spiritually active Yogis, or by those who do not have any kind of direct, and Truth-Revealing, Spiritual experience, or by those who do not truly and rightly understand the Spiritual Revelation of Reality. Truly, yin and yang are merely the polarities of natural energy.

Likewise, sometimes, in some Yogic traditions, the Kundalini Process is interpreted in terms of the conditionally manifested sheaths. Therefore, sometimes, in some Yogic traditions, the error is made of identifying the Divine Shakti-Force with natural processes and energies. This is what I mean when (on occasion) I Say that the Divine Spirit-Force transcends the Kundalini, or that the true Heart-Force (or Hridaya-Shakti) is greater than the Kundalini. In Saying such things, I am criticizing the conventional (or erroneous) interpretation of the Kundalini Shakti, wherein the Kundalini Shakti is identified with one or another species of natural energy.

Truly, <u>only</u> the Spirit Itself is Spiritual. And the real Spiritual Process is the submission of the conditional (or conditionally manifested) bodies (or sheaths), and all experiences and relations of the conditional (or conditionally manifested) bodies (or sheaths), to the Spiritual (and Transcendental, and Divine) Reality, so that they are transcended in (progressively) self-transcending Identification with the Divine Spirit Itself (or the Transcendental and Inherently Spiritual Divine Itself). Ultimately, in the Way of the Heart, the Divine Spirit is Realized to Be Consciousness Itself, Self-Existing and Self-Radiant, Prior to all apparent motions. In the Way of the Heart, in the context of the sixth stage of life, even the causal body (associated with the right side of the heart) is submitted to the Ultimate Spiritual Reality, Which Is Consciousness Itself.

The Awakening to the seventh stage of life in the Way of the Heart is the Realization of Inherent (and Inherently Perfect) Divine Self-Consciousness, inherently transcending conditional existence and all conditionally manifested bodies or forms. In the context of that Awakening, all the five conditionally manifested bodies (or sheaths), and all experiences and relations of these bodies, are inherently (and Divinely) Recognized in Consciousness Itself. Therefore, in the Way of the Heart, in the context of the seventh stage of life (wherein there is already Inherent, and Inherently Perfect, Identification with Transcendental, Inherently Spiritual, and Divine Self-Consciousness), the Inherent Divine Siddhi of Recognition Demonstrates Itself through the progressive Signs of Divine Transfiguration, Divine Transformation, Divine Indifference, and Divine Translation.

These progressive Signs are simply spontaneous expressions of the Inherent Power of Divine Self-Abiding, and, therefore, in due course (in the Way of the Heart), the Demonstration of Divine Recognition simply becomes Divine Indifference.

(In fact, in some cases, there may not be many tangible signs of Divine Transfiguration and Divine Transformation, and, in such cases, the sign of Divine Indifference may occur rather early.)

Ultimately, the Demonstration of the Way of the Heart in the context of the seventh stage of life is that of Perfect Outshining, or Divine Translation, Which is not merely the inherent transcendence (and Recognition) of conditional existence, but the Perfect Outshining of it (without exclusion). Therefore, Divine Translation is the Perfect Outshining of conditional existence itself, in (and by) Consciousness Itself.

The true Spirit-Force is the Inherent Radiance of the Divine Self. And It is not to be equated with any of the mechanics, polarities, or forces of conditional Nature. And It is not to be confused, therefore, with any of the sheaths of the body-mind, or with any experiences associated with them. Nor is the Spirit Itself to be identified with any of the experiences that It appears to stimulate in the various sheaths. The Spirit (or Spirit-Force) is, in Truth, Free, Transcendental, and Divine.

My Spirit-Baptism is simply the Divine Baptism, and It is not to be equated with natural energies or their effects. (This is why I have Said that the true reception of My Spirit-Baptism is not merely a matter of energy experiences, but it is a matter of conversion to Spiritually Awakened Ishta-Guru-Bhakti Yoga, or Spiritually Activated Divine Communion Itself.) Therefore, My Spirit-Baptism is not merely a matter of experiencing energies in the body. In the case of those who (by means of feeling) Contemplate My bodily (human) Form, and My Spiritual (and Always Blessing) Presence, and My Very (and Inherently Perfect) State, what may be perceived (or presumed) to be (usual or unusual) energies (or even Spiritual experiences) in the body are themselves simply the possible effects of My Spiritual (and Always Blessing) Presence on the karmic, or accumulated, limitations of the body itself, or of the body-mind itself, or of the mind itself. Thus, as the Current of My Spiritual (and Always Blessing) Presence pervades (and flows in) the Circle, and the Arrow, of the body-mind, various karmic limitations are stimulated and (if allowed to pass) purified, and this process of stimulation and purification is evidence of My Spiritual (and Always Blessing) Presence at Work (and shown via psycho-physical effects), but My Spirit-Baptism (or My Spiritual, and Always Blessing, Presence Itself) has truly been received only when It sets the heart to Communion with Me (and, Thus and Thereby, with the Ultimate, and Inherently Spiritual, Divine) and converts the apparent individual being (even in all its sheaths) to (fullest and self-transcending) Devotion to Me (and, Thus and Thereby, to Spiritually responsive and responsible surrender to the Transcendental and Inherently Spiritual Divine).

V

The grossest dimension of the body-mind is the physical body itself. It is associated with desire (or motive) and action based on desire. Therefore, the traditional path called Karma Yoga (or renunciation of the purposes and goals of the ego in bodily activity) was developed as a means to transcend bondage to bodily desire and activity (by surrendering the causes and the results of bodily action to the Divine Person and Self-Condition, and this by converting all actions into forms of worship, or, as in the Way of the Heart, into forms of self-surrendering, self-forgetting, and self-transcending Ishta-Guru-Bhakti).

The gross body is, very simply, the food body. The gross body itself depends on (and is made of) food. The quality and quantity of food largely (or very basically) determines the state and desire and action of the physical body and the sense-mind. If food-taking is intelligently minimized, and if the food selected is both pure and purifying, then the physical body (and even the total mind and the emotional dimension of the being) passes through a spontaneous natural cycle that first shows signs of purification, then rebalancing, and, finally, rejuvenation. Therefore, if food-taking is controlled, the physical body itself, including its desires and activities, becomes rather easily (or simply) controllable.

On the basis of this principle, it is very simple (in principle) to restore the gross body to balance, health, and well-being. The basic treatment of any unhealthful condition of the gross body is a food treatment (generally accompanied by rest from, or otherwise right and effective control of, all the enervating influences and effects of daily life). Therefore, primarily, it is through the food-discipline (accompanied by general self-discipline) that gross bodily purification, rebalancing, and rejuvenation are accomplished.

This "food principle" is the fundamental basis of all physical healing. Some bodily conditions may require special healing treatments, but even such special approaches will be useful (in the fullest and long-term sense) only if accompanied by fundamental changes in diet (and simultaneous changes in one's habits of life). Therefore, always, the primary (and right) approach to physical health and physical well-being must be (first) to address (or examine) and (then) to treat (and to discipline) the gross body simply (or directly) as a food process.

If the dietary (and the total) discipline of the body-mind is right, then (in the Way of the Heart) attention can be more fully (or less resistively) Released to Ishta-Guru-Bhakti, and (thus, by Grace) to My Revelation of the Divine Person, and (Thus and Thereby) to the Direct Blessing of the Divine Person (and, in the case of My Spiritually Active devotees, to the Gracefully Revealed and Given and Magnified Blessing-Presence, or the Spirit-Current in, and, ultimately, Prior to, the Circle and the Arrow of the body-mind), and (ultimately, and even from the beginning) to the Mere Presence of the Divine Person (or the Graceful Revelation of Perfectly Subjective Being, Itself). If the dietary discipline of the body-mind and the Devotional feeling-discipline of attention (which discipline corresponds to the tradition of Bhakti Yoga) are right, then all aspects of the gross or frontal personality will be most easily (or most readily) economized and submitted to the Spiritual Process.

The frontal Yoga of the Way of the Heart (or right Devotional submission of the frontal personality) takes place in the context of the fourth stage of life. Therefore, it is a matter of the submission of the gross body and the total frontal personality to the Heart-Principle.

The gross body depends on the various levels of the subtle body (and they, each in turn, depend on one another). Therefore, the gross body relates directly to the first level of the subtle body, which is the body of prana (or natural life-energy).

In fact, the gross bodily person is rooted (or grounded) in the abdominal region, or the general region of the navel (including all functions below the navel). Therefore, once both hearing and seeing are established, the practice of the Way of the Heart becomes (at first) a matter of the frontal Yoga of submitting attention into the (by Grace Revealed) Spirit-Current, so that It may pass (as the Spirit-Current naturally does) from the navel to the center of the heart region. Once the gross or frontal personality is under control (via a complex of disciplines associated with "money, food, and sex", or life-relations, diet, and sexuality[6]), and once the gross frontal dimension of the Spirit-Current is submitted (or followed) to the center of the heart (and steadied at the feeling level or heart chakra), then practice of the Way of the Heart has moved fully from the frontal (or descending) Yoga and (potentially) to the spinal (or ascending) Yoga. And among all the practical, functional, relational, and cultural disciplines that serve this transition (as well as the frontal Yoga itself), the conservative discipline (or control) of diet is (elementally) the most basic (because dietary practice, which controls or largely determines the state of the food body, or the state and general activity of the physical body, also determines the relative controllability of social, sexual, emotional,

---

6. Heart-Master Da Love-Ananda has always summarized the foundation life-disciplines of the first three stages of life with the phrase "money, food, and sex". Food, sex, and money directly relate to the first three koshas, respectively, and therefore to the frontal personality He describes earlier in this Essay.

mental, and all other functional desires and activities).

If diet is controlled, the gross food body is more easily controlled, and all the disciplines of the body-mind will be, to that degree, quickened in their effectiveness. Therefore, in the Way of the Heart, right and optimum dietary discipline is a necessary basic aspect of practice (beginning, progressively, at the student-novice stage, of formal approach to the Way of the Heart, and, subsequently, at the student-beginner stage of formally acknowledged practice of the Way of the Heart), and right and optimum dietary discipline (once it is thoroughly established, in the course of the student-beginner stage of the Way of the Heart) is a necessary basic characteristic of every (following) developmental stage (whether of the technically "fully elaborated" practice or of the technically "simpler", or even "simplest", practice) of the Way of the Heart.

The right and optimum diet is necessarily a conservative diet. In right (or effective) practice of the Way of the Heart, dietary discipline fully serves the submission of personal energy and attention to the Great Process that becomes Spiritual and Transcendental Divine Self-Realization. Therefore, the right and optimum diet should be intelligently moderated in its quantity and carefully selected in its quality, so that it will not burden the physical body or bind the mind, or attention, through food desire. Consequently, right and optimum diet should, as a general rule, be natural, fresh, whole, wholesome, balanced, balancing, pure, or non-toxic, and purifying—or, in the language of tradition, sattvic. And right and optimum diet should, as a general rule, be limited to what is necessary and sufficient for bodily (and general psycho-physical) purification, balance, well-being, and appropriate service.

In the Way of the Heart, right diet is whatever diet is the "Minimum Optimum" diet for good health, well-being, and full practice of the Way of the Heart, in the case of the individual. Therefore, there is no absolute standard diet, applicable to all cases, but there is a basic dietary orientation that should stand as a guide to all. That basic orientation (or general dietary rule) is to eat only raw (and sattvic) foods, unless (or except to the degree that) cooked (sattvic) foods are (in one or another form) necessary for good health and well-being.

In My experience (which is confirmed by tradition and by modern research and experimentation), the basic diet, or the diet that most fully and consistently meets all the requirements for right diet (or the "Minimum Optimum" diet I have indicated), is either an exclusively raw (vegetable and/or fruit) diet or a maximally raw vegetarian (fruit and vegetable) diet (consisting of both raw and cooked foods in varying degrees).[7] In either case, such a basic (or "Minimum Optimum") diet is, as a general rule, limited to fruits, and (perhaps) seeds and nuts, and (perhaps) sprouts, greens, grasses, and other vegetables of choice, including (perhaps) a few root vegetables (such as carrots and beets, and perhaps some cooked, or even raw, potatoes), and also (perhaps) some legumes and grains (sprouted, or even soaked, or perhaps, in moderate amounts, cooked). In the case of such a dietary discipline, foods are taken in both solid and liquid forms (except during fasts, or during any period in which an exclusively liquid fruit, or liquid vegetable, or liquid fruit and vegetable diet is preferred), and the general rule is to take food in moderate amounts, without vitamins or other supplements (unless strictly required), and (as a general rule, consistently applied) without social "accessories" (such as tobacco, or alcohol), and (entirely) without social drugs, and (generally) without stimulants (such as coffee or tea), or junk food, or any food substances that do not qualify as sattvic substances or otherwise correspond to the types or quantities of food ordinarily taken.

During periods of intentional purification, systematic release, and generally reduced intake, such a diet is usually restricted exclusively to raw foods (even in liquid form), and at other times (of constructive increase and general bodily development) some intelligently measured amounts of cooked food

7. The "raw diet" is a working principle of dietary practice rather than an ideal, as Sri Da Avabhasa goes on to elaborate in these pages.

may (as necessary) be taken. Even so, the basic rule of this dietary design is that food should be restricted to raw substances only, typically limited to the general range of possibilities I have described, and without cooked food of any kind, unless (or except to the degree that) some kind and amount of cooked food is found to be necessary for weight maintenance, bodily strength, balanced health (or general and healthful equanimity), and basic vitality and well-being.

In order to understand and evaluate the "Minimum Optimum" dietary discipline (or disciplined dietary practice) Given by Me for application by all practitioners of the Way of the Heart, you should study the total and progressive sattvic dietary approach communicated in My summaries of Instruction relative to dietary discipline.[8] Likewise, as a further aid to your understanding and evaluation of the by Me Given "Minimum Optimum" dietary discipline, you may do well to study the total tradition, including the modern (or latest) research and experimentation, relative to sattvic (or pure and purifying, rebalancing, and rejuvenating) dietary discipline. Then, if you agree with the sattvic dietary approach I have communicated, and if you are prepared to embrace that discipline as your own, begin the progressive development of the right and optimum diet that is best for your particular constitution (or psycho-physical type[9]), and always vary the diet artfully (but within the range of its basic principles),

8. Please see *The Eating Gorilla Comes in Peace: The Transcendental Principle of Life Applied to Diet and the Regenerative Discipline of True Health,* Sri Da Avabhasa's major Text on the practices relating to diet and health in the Way of the Heart.

9. Heart-Master Da Love-Ananda has distinguished three basic psycho-physical types, or strategies, of imbalance relative to bodily existence, which He has called "vital" (characterized by preference for the experiential possibilities of the physical body), "peculiar" (characterized by preference for the experiential possibilities of emotion), and "solid" (characterized by preference for the experiential possibilities of the verbal mind). For Heart-Master Da Love-Ananda's Wisdom-Teaching concerning these three types, see chapter 23 of *The Dawn Horse Testament.*

In general, the "vital" person is likely to need less cooked food and should avoid stimulating foods, the "peculiar" person is likely to need more cooked food and is aided by mildly stimulating foods, and the "solid" person requires a balanced regimen. Although every individual is predominantly characterized by one of these three strategies, the three strategies are not mutually exclusive. Therefore, the effects of more than one strategy may need to be taken into account when using dietary practice to balance the "vital", "solid", and "peculiar" life-strategies.

in response to such factors as climate, the availability of food (and the availability of locally grown food), your level of physical (and mental, and emotional) activity, and your age and stage of life (or the developmental stage of your practice in the Way of the Heart).

Always practice dietary discipline with appropriate medical advice and supervision, so that the pace, the special requirements, and the results of your dietary discipline can be determined most efficiently and organized most effectively.

As a student-beginner in the Way of the Heart (and, originally, as a student-novice, or actively listening applicant for the right to practice the Way of the Heart), begin (unless medically advised otherwise) by embracing (and progressively developing and refining) a basic general vegetarian (fruit and vegetable) diet, which diet should (in the general case) consist of both raw and cooked foods (and, if strictly necessary, some, generally small and occasional, amounts of milk and milk products).[10]

Develop (and refine) your basic dietary practice while you also develop and refine all the other basic (functional, practical, relational, and cultural) requirements for self-discipline in the Way of the Heart[11].

If medical advice permits, your dietary practice should also include (as a basic means to quicken the natural process of purification, rebalancing, and rejuvenation) weekly (or at least occasional) one-day fasts and occasional (or, in some cases, even relatively frequent) long fasts (using one or another combination of pure water, raw fruit juices, raw vegetable juices,

10. In the basic general vegetarian diet for practitioners of the Way of the Heart, all foods should be natural, organic, unprocessed (or minimally and naturally processed), and the freshest available. Practitioners of the Way of the Heart take foods in appropriate combinations, moderate amounts, and at regularly scheduled times.

As every vegetarian knows, "health food" supermarkets now make it quite possible to mimic all the unconscious habits and to pursue the very same egoic satisfactions that typically possess non-vegetarians, while still partaking only of the natural food types given on this list. Consequently, merely to eat "approved" foods is not to take on even the basic general vegetarian diet in any meaningful way. Rather, beginners in the Way of the Heart must make the entire matter of food-taking and associated health issues a sacred practice of observation, intelligence, and appropriate and steadily increasing self-discipline.

11. The primary discipline of practitioners of the Way of the Heart is Satsang, or the practice of "Good Company", specifically in the form of their relationship to Da Avabhasa as Adept Heart-Teacher and True Heart-Master. All disciplines of the Way of the Heart,

vegetable broths, and herb teas, for 7-10 days, or longer), and also periods of raw diet (or raw mono-diet), either in addition to fasting or, if medically necessary, as an alternative to fasting.

Refine (or simplify) your diet progressively, and, thus (but as directly and quickly as possible), pass through the necessary cycles of purification, rebalancing, and rejuvenation, until (in the course of student-beginner practice of the Way of the Heart, as and whenever your health and general state permits) the discipline of either an exclusively raw (vegetable and/or fruit) diet or a maximally raw vegetarian (fruit and vegetable) diet (consisting of both raw and, as necessary, cooked foods, but without the use of milk or milk products), and (in either case) with food taken always in minimum but adequate quantities, is, as a consistent daily rule, stably achieved.

All those who would advance from the student-beginner stage to the intensive listening-hearing stage (whether of the technically "elaborate" or of the technically "simpler", or even "simplest", practice) of the Way of the Heart must (as a prerequisite) naturally exhibit basic psycho-physical equanimity, and they must, therefore, practice optimum dietary purity, simplicity, and moderation (in the general manner I have described). Once the transition is made to the intensive listening-hearing stage of the Way of the Heart, the practice of dietary purity, simplicity, and moderation must (as a consistent daily rule) be continued (even in all the developmental stages beyond the intensive listening-

---

therefore, are lived as forms of the senior discipline of Satsang, or devotional Communion with Heart-Master Da. Thus, practitioners maximize the time they spend in meditative feeling-Contemplation of Sri Da Avabhasa's bodily (human) Form, His Spiritual (and Always Blessing) Presence, and His Very (and Inherently Perfect) State; study of Heart-Master Da's Wisdom-Teaching and the Leelas (or Sacred Stories) of His Revelatory Work; devotional fellowship within the culture of the formal community of practitioners of the Way of the Heart; Spiritual retreat and service, when rightly prepared, at the Retreat Sanctuaries Sri Da Avabhasa has Empowered; and, likewise when properly prepared, reception of His Heart-Transmission in His Personal (physical) Company.

The practical, functional, relational, cultural, and formal community disciplines and obligations in the Way of the Heart apply to diet and health; exercise; sexuality and intimate relationships; work, service, and financial support; cooperative association with other practitioners within the formal community of the Way of the Heart; study; formal devotional meditation, or feeling-Contemplation of Sri Da Avabhasa; sacramental activities; and the "daily form", or schedule of daily activities.

See *The Dawn Horse Testament* for Heart-Master Da Love-Ananda's summary of the basic requirements of student-beginner practice.

hearing stage of the Way of the Heart), and such a practice (once established) will naturally tend to be continued, even in the context of the seventh stage of life (in the Way of the Heart).

Those individuals (at the student-novice stage, of approach to the Way of the Heart, or at the student-beginner stage of practice of the Way of the Heart, or at any developmental stage beyond the student-beginner stage of the Way of the Heart) who are medically (and correctly) advised (or, otherwise, who, because of circumstances of unusually limited availability of sattvic foods of the optimum and highest quality type, are obliged) to maintain a less restricted (or more conventional) diet (either consistently or occasionally, and, if occasionally, either for briefer or for longer periods)—including (perhaps) a great percentage of cooked foods, and (perhaps) milk and milk products (even beyond the earliest phase of adaptation to the, eventually, either exclusively raw or maximally raw vegetable and/or fruit diet), and (perhaps) also eggs, or (perhaps) even flesh food (whether fish, fowl, or animal), and (perhaps) with therapeutic doses of vitamins and other food supplements as well, in addition to the basic diet of grains, legumes, nuts, seeds, and various other vegetables, and also fruits—may, of course, do so (under medical supervision, or otherwise as necessity requires, and, as must be the case relative to even every matter of practice and discipline in the Way of the Heart, always with the formal agreement of the cooperative community culture of all formally acknowledged practitioners of the Way of the Heart), but they should do so without self-indulgence, strictly for health reasons (or otherwise by necessity), and with constant sensitivity (and self-transcending response) to the effects such foods produce in the body-mind, and on personal energy, and on attention. (However, such dietary plans, or necessities, would necessarily be exceptional and unusual, in the Way of the Heart. And, most likely, any such plan, if medically required, would be related to the treatment of either some varieties of disease or of constitutional weakness that, at least temporarily, are not amenable to the optimum sattvic dietary approach.)

In any case, all student-novices, all student-beginners, and all practitioners at any developmental stage beyond the student-beginner stage of the Way of the Heart should entirely avoid social (or recreational) drugs (not only because they are, in most cases and places, illegal, but also, or otherwise, because they are generally self-deluding and degenerative in their effect). Likewise, all student-novices, and all student-beginners in the Way of the Heart, should also (for the same reason, and as a general and consistent daily rule of practice) avoid the use of tobacco, alcohol, coffee, tea, junk food, and the like. And all practitioners of the Way of the Heart who would advance to the intensive listening-hearing stage, or who are already advanced to the intensive listening-hearing stage, or to any developmental stage beyond it, in the Way of the Heart, should, likewise (as a general and consistent daily rule of practice), avoid tobacco, alcohol, coffee, tea, junk food, and the like.

Once any individual has truly and fully adapted to the consistent (daily) practice of optimum dietary purity, simplicity, and moderation, he or she would not often (or, perhaps, ever) choose, or even be able to physically enjoy or easily tolerate, "accessory" substances (such as tobacco, alcohol, coffee, tea, junk food, and the like). Indeed, the Way of the Heart is, even from the beginning (and even in the context of the student-novice stage, of approach to the Way of the Heart), a self-purifying and self-transcending Way of life. Therefore, from the beginning (and also in the context of the student-novice stage, of approach to the Way of the Heart), the complete avoidance of the grossest of "accessory" substances (such as tobacco, or alcohol) is the optimum (and, generally, necessary) practice (except, perhaps, in the rarest and rightest of positively celebratory occasions), and the general and consistent (daily) avoidance of the less gross substances (such as coffee, tea, junk food, sweets and special dishes made with refined sugar, sweets and special dishes made with refined flour, foods manufactured with additives, and so on) is the necessary practice (except, perhaps, in the context of right and occasional celebratory events, or, in the case of tea in particular, in the context of rare occasions that may require a functional stimulant).

The total transition from conventional (or worldly) dietary practice to basic vegetarian (or, if strictly necessary, lacto-vegetarian) dietary practice, and then to a maximally raw vegetarian (fruit and vegetable) dietary practice (optimally, without milk or milk products), and then (perhaps) to an (at least periodically, or even consistently) exclusively raw (vegetable and/or fruit) dietary practice can (and, generally, must) take a significant period of time. Many individuals may be, for one or another physical reason, unable (and not medically advised) to achieve a (consistently, or even more or less regularly) exclusively raw dietary economy (although most individuals should be able to progressively develop a maximally raw vegetarian practice that, as necessary, makes use of cooked food, both fruit and vegetable), but even in the case of those who are physically (and from a medical point of view) able to achieve either an exclusively raw food, or otherwise maximally raw food, practice, the progressive process may rightly take from several months to a year (or, in some cases, even longer), depending on the previous habits, the strength of intention, and the general state of health of the individual.

Those (and only those) who eventually achieve the ability to healthfully maintain a (consistently, or at least more or less regularly) exclusively raw fruit and vegetable diet (and who otherwise maintain a maximally raw fruit and vegetable diet, at those periodic or random times when an exclusively raw fruit and vegetable diet cannot, for one or another physical reason, be maintained) may then, if they choose, extend the experiment of their dietary discipline, until they achieve a diet that is (at least at times) either primarily or exclusively made of raw fruit (perhaps generally including raw fruit-type vegetables), taken in solid form and in the form of juices (or, from time to time, exclusively in the form of juices, even, perhaps, along with various types of raw vegetable juices). Experiments with fruit diet, periodic liquid diet, random and occasional eating, or any other greatly reduced dietary practice should, of course, be carefully monitored by medical professionals, to be certain the results are healthful, but such traditional experiments may be worth trying and testing (by rightly prepared individuals), and such experiments do have a tradition of success (as well as failure, particularly in the case of individuals who did not sufficiently prepare the physical body, the emotional being, and the mind for such profound dietary conservation by preceding it with a gradual and effective program of physical, or total psycho-physical, purification, rebalancing, and rejuvenation).

VI

Every practitioner of the Way of the Heart (beginning at the student-beginner stage, or, as may be the case, beginning even in the context of early-life practice), and also every student-novice (or actively listening applicant for the right to practice the Way of the Heart), should (freely and intelligently) enter the (progressive) dietary ordeal of practice, in which the physical body (or even the total body-mind) is disciplined until it admits only (or the maximum) well-being. Likewise, the conservative principle associated with right dietary discipline should be (progressively) duplicated at every level of functional (or total psycho-physical) life.

Thus, for example, a conservative (and self-transcending) sexual discipline must (in the Way of the Heart) be progressively established.[12] In its most basic form (as simple emotional-

---

12. The sexual discipline of formal practitioners in the Way of the Heart begins with study of Heart-Master Da's Wisdom-Teaching relative to the emotional-sexual ego and right sexual practice, and it is quickly extended via disciplined frequency of sexual intercourse and the primary commitment to observe, understand, and, thereby, transcend emotional dissociation, reactivity, and seeking in all of its moods and manifestations (and emotional-sexual complications or problems altogether). From the inception of their preparatory practice as student-novices, individuals are expected to confine their sexual activity to a committed intimate relationship (whether heterosexual or homosexual). At appropriate moments in their life of practice, devotees specifically "consider" and accept transformative discipline relative to any limitations upon their stylistic freedom and performance of the sexual act, and they develop increasing responsibility for conserving or bypassing degenerative sexual orgasm and for cultivating regenerative sexual orgasm via the "conductivity", or circulation, of the natural energy-field and, in due course, the Spiritual Current.

sexual responsibility, in the form of non-promiscuous, non-casual, and non-excessive sexual behavior), that conservative discipline must be established in the student-novice stage, of formal approach to the Way of the Heart. In its comprehensive basic form (as ever-increasing emotional-sexual responsibility, and, in the case of individuals involved in emotional-sexual intimacy, whether sexually active or sexually inactive, basic "true intimacy", and, in the case of sexually active individuals, the practice of sexual "conscious exercise" and the fullest necessary conservative management of the frequency of sexual intercourse), that conservative discipline must (progressively) become characteristic of the practice of every adult individual at the student-beginner stage of the Way of the Heart (and continue thereafter to be characteristic of the practice of every adult practitioner of the Way of the Heart, until the individual completes the would-be-seeing, or progressively seeing, stage of the Way of the Heart). And, once any individual enters the first actually seeing stage (or any developmental stage beyond it) in the Way of the Heart, either formal "celibate renunciation" or "true intimacy" (including either "sexual communion", conservatively managed relative to frequency of sexual intercourse, or else celibacy) is the sexual discipline that should characterize the practice of the Way of the Heart. (And the practice of conservative dietary discipline does a great deal to establish the necessary equanimity in the body-mind that makes stable conservative sexual discipline both naturally simple and easeful.)

"True intimacy" is not merely conventional or socially sanctioned coupling. "True intimacy" is the sadhana (or Spiritual and Yogic discipline) of <u>love</u> (in the context of relationships between emotional-sexual intimates, whether or not those intimates are sexually active). Ego-based sexuality tends toward loveless, casual eroticism and repetitive sexual activity for the sake of stress-release. The Way of the Heart involves an Ordeal of real self-understanding, whereby practitioners progressively transcend the egoic (or self-contracted) sexual motive. Thus, when any individual enters the first actually seeing stage of the

Way of the Heart, either formal "celibate renunciation" or (fully developed) "true intimacy" should become a certain choice (based on most fundamental self-understanding), and the true Yoga of "sexual communion" should then (in the case of sexually active devotees) be developed during the first actually seeing stage (and the later developmental stages of practice).

"True intimacy" is Spiritually positive love-intimacy, with or without sexual activity, expressed in the form of real, and, therefore, potentially long-term, or even lifelong, commitment in relationship. "True intimacy" is a practice (not a contract, and not the mere fact of any particular relationship). "True intimacy" is something to do, not something to have.

"True intimacy" is generally (or typically, but not necessarily in every case) engaged with only one partner (during any particular period of an individual's life), but only because of the human and Spiritual demands of "true intimacy" itself, and not because monogamy is the "ideal". Monogamy itself is simply a social convention (associated with some, and not all, traditional societies), and it is largely based on the economic and political patterns of pre-industrial civilization. Likewise, legal, or State-sanctioned, marriage is a legal and social convention, and it is a logical extension of all the pre-industrial economic and political techniques traditionally used to maintain (or enforce) common order. Indeed, State-sanctioned marriage, whether monogamous or polygamous, is basically a sex-restrictive social device for controlling and monitoring human reproduction, and thus the ownership and orderly transference of property, so that taxation and the power of ownership have a logical basis, but this subjugation of emotional-sexual relationships to the presumed needs or necessities of the State becomes less and less tenable in post-industrial societies, where emotional-sexual relationships and activities have achieved, and positively serve, a more recreational than reproductive purpose. Therefore, as post-industrial emotional-sexual practices develop (or more and more allow) new, truly re-creational (or rejuvenative), and even evolutionary (or Spiritual) purposes, and as post-industrial societies develop new means for handling practical requirements, such as taxation (and the designation of property ownership), without attaching (or otherwise manipulating and suppressing) the emotional-sexual relationships of free citizens, State-sanctioned marriage becomes more an option than a standard practice.

Conventions (or common group expectations relative to individual behavior) are not absolutes, nor are any of them universally affirmed or practiced. Likewise, conventions change, and there are always exceptions to any rule. And, in particular, human emotional-sexual possibilities are always better served by human freedom, human love, and True Heart-Wisdom (Awakened in the context of real Spiritual culture and practice) than by merely public restraints. Therefore, in the Way of the Heart, emotional-sexual relationships (whatever their specific form or pattern may be in any particular time, place, or personal circumstance) are "considered" only in terms of the practice of "true intimacy", or the simplicity that is intimate commitment itself. (And My description of "true intimacy" necessarily contains no reference to legal contracts, because legal and otherwise "civilized" conventions have no fundamental association with intimacy itself.)

Love itself cannot rightly be patterned or sanctioned for "civilized" purposes, and sex itself wills not to be legalized or "civilized" (or controlled by any external means). Only the ego (both collective and individual) tries to "civilize" love and sex by arbitrary (or Heartless) ideals, rules, and implications. In the Way of the Heart, egoity itself is (at least progressively) transcended, and love and sex are (especially in the seeing devotee's practice of "sexual communion") re-unified in a self-transcending Yoga of Divine Communion. Therefore, in the Way of the Heart, "true intimacy" (once established) is generally (or most typically) engaged with only one partner (during any particular period of an individual's life), but simply (or realistically) because most individuals do not (and it is not in any sense necessary for them to) have sufficient personal energy and attention to practice the profoundly demanding Yoga of "true intimacy" and "sexual communion" with more than one partner at a time.

More and more people in post-industrial societies practice serial marriage (or serial polygamy), or (in rarer cases) even concurrent polygamy (or simultaneous multiple sexual relationships). That is to say, in the course of their lifetime, many, if not most, individuals in post-industrial societies engage in a number of marriages, or significant emotional-sexual intimacies, including both long-term and short-term commitments. Therefore, in the Way of the Heart, practitioners are simply Called to observe and to understand and to transcend merely egoic, or self-contracted and separative, motives in the context of emotional-sexual practice, in order to <u>maximize</u> intimate commitment and (in the case of truly seeing devotees) in order to conserve the Spirit-Current and serve the self-transcending Spiritual Process of Transcendental Divine Realization.

Practitioners in the Way of the Heart are not Called to conform to any conventional "ideal", but they are only Called to the Heart Itself. Indeed, if Truth (rather than egoity) is the "point of view", all conventional or merely idealistic expectations relative to the pattern or design of personal sexuality must ultimately be replaced by a Free Spiritual culture of individual responsibility in love. (Therefore, in the progressive development of the Way of the Heart, "true intimacy" can, in principle, be practiced by homosexual devotees just as well as by heterosexual devotees, for it is just as difficult, or ego-transcending, to practice "true intimacy" and "sexual communion" as an intelligent and emotionally responsible homosexual as it is to do so as an intelligent and emotionally responsible heterosexual.)

"Sexual communion" is a Yoga that can be truly practiced <u>only</u> in love. (In the Way of the Heart, "sexual communion" is not merely a traditional and ego-based sex-technique.) And "sexual communion" should become a discipline that is only appropriately, and not casually, engaged. Thus, in the Way of the Heart, devotees (at the first actually seeing stage, and beyond) who practice "sexual communion" (and also all earlier stage practitioners of the Way of the Heart who practice sexual conservation and sexual "conscious exercise") should maintain the Sila (or conservative discipline) of limiting their sexual activity to those specific occasions when each partner is physically, emotionally, and mentally prepared for sexual intimacy (and, in the case of seeing devotees, altogether Spiritually prepared for fully right practice of the sexual Yoga of Love-Communion with by Grace Revealed Love-Bliss Itself).

Maintained by every right means, a daily life generally free of (and, in some cases, even generally secluded from) emotional-sexual interaction (or casual emotional-sexual distraction), and, altogether, a daily life full of one-pointed Devotion to Me, allows each individual practitioner of the Way of the Heart to maintain the necessary integrity of his or her own physical and psychic sphere, and of his or her own daily Devotional practice of the Way of the Heart. Thus, typically, every formal "celibate renunciate" should share daily living quarters (and daily sleeping quarters) with other formal "celibate renunciates" who are members only of their same sex (although, in cases, or at times, of unique developmental demonstration, and the capability for making a uniquely effective use of solitude, a private room, or a private dwelling place, may be appropriate). Likewise, and even as an aid to the Sila of rightly choosing emotional-sexual occasions, intimately practicing devotees in the Way of the Heart should, optimally, if their physical and personal circumstances permit (or, in some cases, as their formal practice obligations may require), maintain, as a general daily rule, separate sleeping quarters (or, at least, separate beds). Thus, if they maintain daily sleeping arrangements somehow apart from one another, intimately practicing devotees in the Way of the Heart must appropriately choose specific occasions, of appropriate frequency, for sexual intimacy, or, otherwise, simply for holding one another and sleeping together, in one or another place chosen, and perhaps even reserved, for that special purpose. Just so, within the context of cooperative community, even all My devotees should, optimally, if their physical and personal circumstances permit (or, in some cases, as their formal practice obligations may require), and, altogether, for the sake of maintaining one-pointed devotion to Me, share daily sleeping quarters with other devotees who are members only of their same sex (while, of course, otherwise allowing for appropriately arranged occasions, and appropriately arranged alternative places, for contact between emotional-sexual intimates). And, perhaps on a general daily basis, or at least on an occasional and more or less extended basis, as, for instance, when engaged in meditative retreat, even all My devotees should share both daily living quarters and daily sleeping quarters with, and generally reside in the collective environments, and in the one-pointed Devotional company, of, devotees who are members only of their same sex (although, especially during periods of meditative retreat, a private room, or a private dwelling place, may be appropriate, in cases, or at times, of unique developmental demonstration and the capability for making uniquely effective use of solitude).

Inappropriately frequent sexual activity (at any developmental stage of practice in the Way of the Heart, or even in the student-novice stage, of formal approach to the Way of the Heart) should not be indulged, or else sexual activity tends merely to become a cause and a result of emotional-sexual (and general physical, and psycho-physical) imbalance, as well as the cause and the result of a lack of discrimination in mind. Therefore, in the Way of the Heart, right Sila relative to "sexual communion" (and also relative to sexual conservation and sexual "conscious exercise") generally (and typically) involves a discipline relative to frequency (of sexual activity) itself.

For sexually active student-beginners in the Way of the Heart (and, at least to a significant basic degree, for sexually active student-novices, formally approaching the Way of the Heart), and also for sexually active practitioners in the intensive listening-hearing stage of the Way of the Heart, and sexually active practitioners in the would-be-seeing (or progressively seeing) stage of the Way of the Heart, the right practice of sexual conservation (and sexual "conscious exercise", once and after such begins to develop in the context of student-beginner practice of the Way of the Heart) requires a discipline relative to the frequency of sexual occasion, and also relative to the frequency of degenerative orgasm, and such frequencies will vary according to the observed effects of these on the total practice of the Way of the Heart (or, otherwise, on the general quality of the student-novice approach to the Way of the Heart) in the case of the particular individuals involved. (Therefore, relative to these matters, I have Given both general and particular indications in My summary of Instruction relative to emotional-sexual discipline, as Given for application by practitioners of the Way of the Heart, and, in a rudimentary and preparatory manner, for minimum application, and general study-"consideration", by student-novices, formally approaching formally acknowledged practice of the Way of the Heart. And I have also, in that summary of Instruction, Given specific indications relative to restraint during the would-be-seeing, or progressively seeing, stage of the Way of the Heart.)[13]

For those who choose to be sexually active during the first actually seeing stage of the Way of the Heart (and at any developmental stage of practice beyond the first actually seeing stage of the Way of the Heart), "sexual communion" should be the practice in every sexual occasion. And, in the first actually seeing stage of the Way of the Heart, right Sila relative to the frequency of sexual occasion (and thus of "sexual communion") should, as a general rule (except in rare cases), limit the frequency of "sexual communion" to no more than once (or perhaps twice) per week (and an even lesser frequency may be found to be appropriate and even necessary in many, if not most, cases). Likewise, the frequency of sexual occasion (and "sexual communion") should, as a general rule (in most cases), become even more limited once practice begins (as it may,

---

13. For Sri Da Avabhasa's summary Instructions on the emotional-sexual disciplines at every developmental stage of the Way of the Heart, please see chapter 21 of *The Dawn Horse Testament*.

possibly) in the "advanced" (or ascending) developmental stage of the fourth stage of life in the Way of the Heart, and then continues in the (possible) context of the fifth stage of life and/or the (necessary) context of the sixth stage of life (which may otherwise be entered directly from the point of maturity in the first actually seeing stage of the Way of the Heart). Thus, in the context of the "advanced" fourth stage of life in the Way of the Heart, sexual occasion (and "sexual communion") should (in most cases) generally (or on the average) be limited to a maximum frequency of between once per month and (perhaps) once per week. And (in most cases) either celibacy (at least for significantly prolonged periods) or else a (perhaps) very much reduced frequency of sexual occasion (and "sexual communion"), to a maximum of once, or perhaps twice, per month (and even less often in many cases) should (as a general rule) be the typical sexual discipline in the full context of practice of the Way of the Heart associated with the fifth and/or the sixth stage of life.

In the Way of the Heart, a <u>relative</u> <u>few</u> individuals may be uniquely suited for a Yogic sexual sadhana[14] (and, thus, for uniquely effective, and truly self-transcending, practice of "sexual communion", whether in the context of the fourth, the fifth, or the sixth stage of life). And some (but not necessarily all) such individuals may (by virtue of the combination of a rare psycho-physical constitution and a profound concentration of responsive counter-egoic effort) be capable of a sexual pattern that <u>rightly</u> allows, at least at times, more frequent participation

14. In *The Dawn Horse Testament,* Sri Da Avabhasa Says that such individuals are uniquely qualified by virtue of "their Exceptional sexual Strength, the Consistent Effectiveness Of their Right Conservative and Regenerative sexual Discipline, their Characteristic Freedom From The Tendency To Collapse From The Feeling-Contemplative, and, Progressively, Spiritual, Transcendental, and Divine, Orientation In The Midst Of a sexually active life, their Characteristic Adherence To The Strictly Yogic and self-Surrendering and God-Realizing Attitude In The Midst Of a sexually active life, their Characteristic Freedom From the idealistic attitude, the romantic attitude, the puritanical attitude, and any and every other merely conventional, or limiting and ego-Reinforcing, attitude In The Midst Of a sexually active life, their Uncommon Demonstration Of self-Discipline, self-Observation, self-Understanding, and effective self-Transcendence Relative To All Aspects Of their emotional-sexual character and Practice, and, Altogether, their General Maturity As Truly Both Hearing <u>and</u> Seeing Practitioners Of The Way Of The Heart".

in "sexual communion" than would be appropriate for others. In such cases, the Yogic transformation of sexual feeling and the regenerative Yogic conversion of the degenerative tendencies of the frontal being are <u>exceptionally</u> effective (in daily life, in meditation, and during "sexual communion"). Those who are not so constituted (or thus concentrated) must, if they are sexually active, be always mindful to conserve the frequency of "sexual communion", and some may do well to practice free (or truly motiveless) celibacy[15] (on the basis of real and most fundamental self-understanding).

The general pattern of either sexual activity or sexual inactivity (or celibacy) developed in the advanced and the ultimate stages of life (through the sixth stage of life) in the Way of the Heart will naturally tend to continue in the context of the seventh stage of life in the Way of the Heart. (However, in the Free context of the seventh stage of life in the Way of the Heart, the apparent intention behind any previously established pattern of sexual activity will, at least eventually, tend to decrease, and the pattern itself will, thereby, tend to become progressively ever more conservative in its frequency, even, ultimately, to the degree of motiveless celibacy.) In any case, even though a rightly conservative sexual practice (whether sexually active or sexually inactive) will, because of real and effective previous sexual sadhana, naturally (or as a psychophysical inevitability) be associated with the Demonstrations of My devotees who Realize the seventh stage of life in the Way of the Heart, no specific (or particular) pattern of sexual (or

15. Since sexuality is so obviously an area of human obsession and bondage, traditional and conventional Spiritual traditions typically recommend or require celibacy from committed practitioners. In such traditions, celibate relinquishment of sexual interest and action is a motivated, goal-oriented choice that hopes and expects that the attention and energy thus liberated from sexuality will be rededicated to Spiritual practice.

In the Way of the Heart, celibacy is not regarded to be either superior or inferior to sexual activity. It is simply a possibility that is to be assumed and practiced as a matter of individual choice based on self-observation, self-understanding, and a liberal desire to magnify one's Contemplative Communion with Heart-Master Da Avabhasa. The primary criterion for all action in the Way of the Heart is that it be immediately self-transcending and God-Realizing. Thus, "motiveless" celibacy (and "motiveless" performance of any action whatsoever) becomes possible when there is stable awakening, through hearing and seeing, to the practice in the "basic" context of the fourth stage of life in the Way of the Heart.

any other kind of) behavior, and no convention of predictable or expected sexual (or any other kind of) behavior, and no display of unconventional or unpredictable or unexpected sexual (or any other kind of) behavior, in itself characterizes or otherwise defines (or limits) the Inherently Perfect Realization That Is the Great Characteristic of the seventh stage of life in the Way of the Heart.

The practice of "sexual communion" conserves the Spirit-Current bodily, but any form of sexual practice, however conservative, can confine (or tend to confine) the mind (and thus attention) to some significant degree. Therefore, transcendence of the confinement of mind (or the bondage of attention) in sexual activity is the true essence of "sexual communion", and, in the case of most seeing devotees (in the first actually seeing stage, and beyond it, in the Way of the Heart), this essence generally expresses itself not only through "sexual communion" itself, but through regular and progressive limitation of the frequency of sexual intercourse. Likewise, that essence may become the choice to maintain significant periods of celibacy (particularly in the context of the fifth stage of life and the sixth stage of life, in the Way of the Heart), and that same choice may also lead to an eventual (and perhaps early) affirmation of permanent (and motiveless, or goal-free) celibacy.

I Call upon all practitioners of the Way of the Heart to practice sexual self-understanding, and also (if they are sexually active) conservative sexual discipline (progressively including varieties of specific and, potentially, Yogic sexual disciplines). Such sexual self-understanding and conservative sexual discipline may not soon (or ever, in life) become permanent celibacy, but (together) they must certainly become sexual "conscious exercise", and (more and more) "true intimacy", and (eventually) "sexual communion", and they must (beginning, progressively, in the context of student-beginner practice of the Way of the Heart) become a discipline of the quality, the frequency, and the effects of sexual activity (including, eventually, of "sexual communion" itself).

Thus, in the Way of the Heart, sexual self-understanding and conservative sexual discipline will (and must necessarily) become either an intelligent and self-transcending choice of celibacy or an equally intelligent, self-transcending, and truly conservative practice of sexual "conscious exercise", and (in due course) "sexual communion", that typically, in most cases, allows, at each of the developmental stages of practice in which it is engaged in the Way of the Heart, only the limited frequency of sexual intercourse I have indicated.

Now that I have Completed (and Spontaneously Retired from) the Ordeal of My Teaching Work,[16] and I Stand Free, Blessing all by My Mere and Blessing Presence, and I am no longer Obliged (or Assuming the Self-Obligation) to Submit body and mind to be in the likeness of worldly seekers and immature practitioners (in order to Instruct them from My Heart), I must also Transmit the Lesson of that Ordeal to all. Therefore, I must emphasize that My own hard-won experience (including many years of Observing, Instructing, and Struggling with would-be practitioners of the Way of the Heart) has proven to Me that the principle of the conservation (or conservative discipline) of sexuality is a necessary one, and it must not be taken casually, or lightly, nor is it to be only occasionally, or only eventually, practiced.

16. Sri Da Avabhasa's spontaneous Retirement from His Teaching Work occurred as a result of a momentous Event at Sri Love-Anandashram, Fiji, on January 11, 1986, which dramatically transformed the character of His Spiritual and Transcendental Work with His devotees and the world.

Previous to that Event, Sri Da Avabhasa had been engaged in Teaching Work for sixteen years (1970-1986), and during that time He had utilized every dimension and function of His own gross and subtle body and mind to develop Instructive and Revelatory Lessons for His devotees. By literally Identifying with them (and thus becoming their likeness completely), He was able to reflect their egoic qualities and preoccupations to themselves.

Despite His extraordinary Service, however, Heart-Master Da's own devotees did not respond to His Miraculous Divine Grace and Wisdom-Teaching by seriously practicing the Way of the Heart thus Revealed to them. In despair over the lack of response to His Teaching Ordeal, on the morning of January 11, 1986, Heart-Master Da bore the apparent signs of death. When His life signs were spontaneously and fully regenerated moments later, His own body and mind were now utterly conformed to His Divine State of Self-Existing and Self-Radiant Being Itself. In the extraordinary Yogic transformation that occurred, Heart-Master Da Avabhasa relinquished the functional vehicles in body and mind through which He had performed His previous Teaching Work.

Now, by virtue of His utterly self-Surrendered Identification with the Divine Self, Heart-Master Da's own bodily (human) Form has become a Perfectly Unobstructed Sign and Agent of the Divine Person, the Means of His Blessing Work for the sake of all beings.

The social demands (or conventional social influences) of the common and mostly humanized, secularized, urbanized, and everywhere "Westernized" world seem to make the Omega-like choice to be a sexually active sexual being nearly inevitable, and with that choice comes a long and profound struggle with all the complications of body, mind, and relationships that characterize the worldly life. That whole enterprise can eventually be converted into Yoga. (I assumed the necessity to do so in My own case, not merely because I was born in the West and was adapted to life as a Westerner, but also, and primarily, because I was Heart-Required to be prepared to Teach, and, therefore, to Submit to identify with, to convert in My own case, and thereby, and also by Means of all My Blessing Work, eventually to convert in others, the ordinary tendencies and purposes that characterize even all people, from all over the world.) Even so, the conversion (or redirecting) of mind (or attention) and sexually motivated personal energy into the Greater Process of a Yogic Spiritual practice that is compatible with every advanced and ultimate stage of life and practice in the Way of the Heart requires a most profound Ordeal of self-understanding and self-transcendence.

If the actual and direct Realization of the Spiritual and Transcendental Divine Person (and Self-Condition) becomes one's felt necessity and surest purpose, then the most direct Process of Realization should be immediately embraced. Why choose a habit of living that does not serve such Realization, and serve It most directly? Why delay the course or encumber the body-mind with desires and attachments that must, in any case, eventually be relinquished? It is true that the Yoga of "sexual communion" can (or may) become fully compatible with the Processes of the Way of the Heart in the context of the advanced and the ultimate stages of life (even the seventh stage of life). Even so, for some, the intelligent and free choice of motiveless celibacy is the optimum (and even the necessary) course.

Many practitioners of the Way of the Heart may discover, even after a long struggle to understand themselves and to overcome their self-bound sexual motivations, that they are still beginners in the Way of the Heart itself, and that they are wrapped up in a mass of ordinary life-obligations as well. And when this serious self-appraisal finally develops (and the effective impulse toward advanced and ultimate practice begins to move the heart), the individual must then (in the midst of an already encumbered life) achieve (or embrace) the disposition of a renunciate and abandon all of the obstructive and complicating aspects of the sexually oriented habit of living.

The whole Process of practice of the Way of the Heart can be much more direct, and much easier (at least by comparison to struggle within the worldly social context), and much quicker than most practitioners tend to suppose (or propose). All that is required is the most intelligent (or rightly and fully "considered") choice (which can, and should, originate, and first develop in practice, in the student-beginner stage of the Way of the Heart, and which should then develop further in practice, in the context of the intensive listening-hearing stage, and beyond it, in the Way of the Heart). And that most intelligent (or rightly and fully "considered") choice is (necessarily) the choice to practice the most conservative possible discipline appropriate for one's own characteristic body-mind.

Right practice is not a matter of choosing the Alpha-like orientation, rather than the Omega-like orientation. All conventional strategies, both Oriental and Occidental, should be transcended in the process of self-understanding. Even so, right practice is necessarily self-transcending. Therefore, in the Way of the Heart, right practice should, as a general rule of daily practice, be conservative relative to the body-mind, and (in the case of all practitioners of the Way of the Heart) unlimited relative to the Process of Ishta-Guru-Bhakti (and, Thus and Thereby, of Devotional Submission of the ego-"I" to the Spiritual and Transcendental Divine Person and Self-Condition). The Alpha strategy merely dissociates from the body-mind and the world. The Omega strategy is simply possessed by the body-mind and the world. Right practice directly transcends the limiting capability of the body-mind and the world, through the process of self-understanding, self-discipline, and self-transcending Divine Communion. Such right practice is neither world-denying (nor self-destructive) nor self-indulgent. It is (more and more) a matter of equanimity (neither attached nor detached) in the face of whatever arises, and (ultimately) it is a matter of utter (self-transcending) Devotion to the (by Grace Revealed) Spiritual and Transcendental Divine Person and Self-Condition, whether or not anything arises.

Therefore, relative to the matter of sexual discipline, the best (or most direct and auspicious and effective) course is the one that most fully expresses the disposition of equanimity (or freedom from both attachment and detachment). Right sexual discipline is more a matter of the understanding and the direct or immediate transcendence of the binding motives associated with sexual activity than it is a matter of any specific kind of sexual activity (or any otherwise strategic effort to overcome sexual activity itself). Even so, right and truly self-transcending sexual discipline, whatever individual form it takes, must necessarily be conservative, if sexual self-understanding and sexual self-transcendence and (ultimately) the self-transcending surrender of attention to the (by Grace Revealed) Spiritual and Transcendental Divine Person and Self-Condition are to be truly profound and complete.

All practitioners of the Way of the Heart must first (and truly) understand themselves (most fundamentally, and in every aspect, including their emotional-sexual character). And those who thus (progressively) become prepared to fully practice "true intimacy" must also, if they are sexually active, progressively demonstrate the conservative discipline of sexuality itself, at first through progressive sexual conservation (or the disciplining of the quality, the frequency, and the general effects of sexual activity), and then through sexual "conscious exercise", and (in the later course) through "sexual communion".

All practitioners of the Way of the Heart must progressively demonstrate sexual self-transcendence (eventually demonstrated either by a conservative and Spiritually auspicious sexually active discipline or else by the profound simplicity of motiveless, and Spiritually auspicious, celibacy). And some practitioners of the Way of the Heart may eventually (if specifically qualified) practice the Way of the Heart as formal "celibate renunciates" (and, thus, live entirely apart from either sexually active or sexually inactive emotional-sexual relationships).

Perhaps, in the everywhere "Westernized" social order, a style of life based on the householder tradition (eventually coupled with the real practice of "true intimacy") is, for many (or even most) practitioners, the most readily practical basis for developing and maintaining life-requirements. Even so, household living (and, ultimately, "true intimacy"), however it is arranged in the larger social context, can and should be based on heart-commitment and on an agreement to serve the Great Process of Spiritual and Transcendental Divine Realization in the case of each partner (and in the case of all others who are served by each partner). And such household living (and, ultimately, full "true intimacy", or Spiritually positive intimacy) can easily be based on agreements of conservative discipline.

It should be clear that I Call all practitioners of the Way of the Heart to rightly conserve (or, in some cases, even to relinquish) sexual attention and sexual activity. The simplest intelligent sexual discipline is to observe sexual motivation and sexual activity, understand exactly how it is a modification and a limitation of Inherent Happiness (or an effort of self-contraction), and, simply by that Process of self-observation and self-transcending understanding, to release (or be set free of) the effort and the degenerative (or attention-binding) intention of sexual thought, sexual speech, sexual feeling, and bodily sexual activity. On that basis, unless a celibate (or, eventually, even a formal "celibate renunciate") life-practice is chosen, the practice of sexual conservation, sexual "conscious exercise", (progressively) "true intimacy" (or right intimate commitment), and (in the later course) "sexual communion" is the inevitable choice.

All such (conservative) choices require the (progressive)

83

demonstration of freedom from the self-binding sexual (and emotional-sexual) motion of attention, in thought, speech, and bodily action. And all such conservative choices, when combined with a strictly conservative dietary discipline, and also with appropriately managed social and service disciplines, will (when applied within the total context of all My Gifts, and Callings, and Disciplines) allow the body-mind, and personal energy (or feeling), and attention to move most directly (and as quickly as possible) to and through the progressive developmental stages of practice in the Way of the Heart.

Ultimately, What Is Realized Is Self-Sufficient Love-Bliss, or Inherent Happiness, Expressed As Real Freedom and Love (or the "equal eye" of Blessing) toward all beings. Therefore, in order to honor and serve this Realization, all aspects of "money, food, and sex" should be intelligently, progressively, and motivelessly conserved and minimized. Such is the orientation of the practical discipline of the body-mind in the Way of the Heart.

Therefore, I Call all practitioners of the Way of the Heart (beginning at the student-beginner stage) and all would-be practitioners of the Way of the Heart (formally approaching, via the student-novice discipline) to (progressively) embrace the truly conservative discipline of the body-mind. Every one should (progressively) conserve and minimize the requirements and activities of the body-mind, to the degree necessary and sufficient for well-being, balance, appropriate service, clarity in meditation, the effective exercise of every aspect of Ishta-Guru-Bhakti, and (in the case of seeing devotees) full submission of personal energy and attention to the (by Grace Revealed) Process of Spiritually Activated Divine Communion and the Great Process of Realization, by Grace, of the Transcendental (and Inherently Spiritual) Divine Self-Condition.

VII

As practice of Ishta-Guru-Bhakti Yoga in the context of the frontal Yoga matures, the discipline of the pranic body begins (or may begin) to develop in the context of the spinal (or ascending) Yoga. Then the practice (still in the context of the fourth stage of life) begins to advance above the gross food body. Thus, when the Spirit-Current is more and more steadied at the heart (and not tending so fiercely to drive below, to the navel region, or the domain of "money, food, and sex"), then the Yoga becomes (or may become) one of submitting the subtle pranic body (or the personal body of life-energy) to the ascending course of the Spirit-Current and the subtle domain of mind.

The food body (or the Spirit-Current in the gross body) is grounded at the navel and centered (or rooted) in feeling and the heart. Therefore, the gross body must be submitted into the Spirit-Current until the Spirit-Current stabilizes at the heart. This is the task of the frontal Yoga and the total Process associated with the fourth stage of life. Just so, the pranic body (or the natural energy that enlivens the gross body) is grounded (and ultimately centered or rooted) at the heart (or the emotional or feeling center), and it is functionally centered in the cycle of breathing (which is associated with the throat center). Therefore, a fundamental key to the (potential) Process associated with the transition from the fourth to the fifth stage of life is the ascent of the Spirit-Current (or attention in the Spirit-Current) from the middle region of the heart to the throat region.

Just as the basic (elemental) discipline that controls the gross food body is the discipline of diet, the basic discipline that controls the pranic body (or the bodily life-energy) is the Spiritual (and Devotional) discipline of breath, or "conductivity" of the Spirit-Current, which is engaged during the would-be-seeing (or progressively seeing) stage (and beyond it) in the Way of the Heart. That discipline develops first in the context of the frontal line (and the frontal personality), and then (at least potentially) it develops (or may develop) in the context of the spinal line (and the ascending Yoga, which includes the feeling-submission of attention in ascent, from the gross bodily domain to the subtle domain of mind). And that portion of the Way of the Heart that relates to both the descending and the (possible) ascending discipline of the body, the breath, and feeling-attention in the Spirit-Current corresponds to the traditional Hatha Yoga, which also develops (or may develop) on the base of Karma Yoga and Bhakti Yoga, and which goes through and beyond a range of bodily and mental disciplines, until it Realizes the fullest discipline of mind, or Raja Yoga.

The practical, functional, relational, and cultural discipline of the body-mind at every developmental stage of any and every by Me Given form of practice, up to and through the first actually seeing stage of the Way of the Heart, is (at the elemental, or gross, level) built upon the primary discipline of diet (which makes possible the effective discipline of bodily activity, service, relationships, sex, and so forth). This (elemental) discipline of diet (and its associated disciplines at the navel and below) is necessarily to be combined with (progressively developing) Ishta-Guru-Bhakti Yoga and with the discipline of breath (coupled with contemplative and meditative feeling-submission of separate self to My bodily human Form, My Spiritual, and Always Blessing, Presence, and My Very, and Inherently Perfect, State, and, Thus and Thereby, and progressively, into the Spiritual Heart-Current and Very Being of the Divine). If this practice (which requires Devotional discipline and responsive surrender of the body-mind and attention) is engaged fully, then transition beyond the first actually seeing stage of the Way of the Heart (and, in general, directly to practice of the Way of the Heart in the context of the sixth stage of life) readily occurs. And it is in the context of the "advanced" fourth stage of life in the Way of the Heart (which developmental stage is to be engaged only by those relative few practitioners in whom the subtle tendencies of mind are unusually strong) that attention in the Spirit-Current ascends from the gross displays at the navel and below and becomes steady, first at the feeling heart of love (signifying Release of the motive of self-contraction in the domain of the navel and the gross body), and then at the throat (in deep meditation, where the breath is quieted and attention is in the Spirit-Current and the mind, rather than in bodily concerns). It is only after the disciplines of the food body (and diet) and the pranic body (and breath) have, along with feeling-submission of self into My Spiritual (and Always Blessing) Presence, steadied breath and body (by the ascending Process) at the throat (and thus in deep meditation) that the Spiritual Process moves (or may move) above, into the subtler reaches of mind.

VIII

Just as the gross food body (or the Spirit-Current at the navel and below) must (in the ascending Process) be submitted into the Spirit-Current at the heart (where body and bodily energy are connected to feeling and breathing), and the pranic body (or the sheath of natural energy that connects body, emotion, and mind) must be submitted into the Spirit-Current at the throat, so also the lower mental body (or the mental function that connects attention to mind-forms, or the psyche, and then to breath, emotion, and body) is the seat where (potentially) the body, emotion, bodily energy, and breath are to be stabilized.

The manomayakosha, or lower mind, is composed of the conscious mind, the subconscious mind, and the unconscious mind. The conscious mind is in the eyes, or the waking brain. The function of the lower mind reaches down (via the throat) to become the subconscious mind, and it reaches further down (via the navel) to become the unconscious mind. (The "unconscious mind" I refer to here is not "the totality of the Unknown", or the totality of whatever is presently outside the focus of attention, including the superconscious mind, and even Transcendental Consciousness Itself, but it is simply the lower depth of mind, associated with the lower or vital functions, or the navel region, of the personality.) Dreaming is typically associated with the subconscious mind and the unconscious mind. Therefore, dreaming is commonly associated with the regions of the throat and the navel. However, superconscious dreams or visions may also arise, and these are associated with the higher mind and, therefore, with the bodily region, or brain mechanisms, between and above the brows. (Deep sleep is not associated with the unconscious mind, but with the causal deep, in which the mind is inactive, or latent, but not utterly or permanently dissolved. It, like Transcendental Self-Realization, is entered via a Process associated with the right side of the heart.)

When (in the ascending Process) control of the gross body (principally through dietary control) and control of breath (and feeling-attention in the, by Grace Revealed, Spirit-Current) have stabilized at the heart and then the throat, great mental and bodily equanimity is Realized, so that attention may easily reach and rest at the Ajna Door (or the brain core, deep behind and between and slightly above the brows). When the otherwise wandering energies of the conscious mind (and thus also of the subconscious mind and the unconscious mind, which are below the conscious mind and dependent on the conscious mind) are collected at the single point of the Ajna Door, then attention has reached the Doorway to the superconscious mind, and the Process of the ascent of mind. Therefore, profound and easy and steady concentration of attention in the Inherent Love-Bliss of the Spirit-Current at the Ajna Door is the sign that indicates the completion of the "advanced" fourth stage of life in the Way of the Heart.

IX

The fifth stage of life in the Way of the Heart (which, like the "advanced" fourth stage of life in the Way of the Heart, is to be engaged by those relative few practitioners in whom the subtle tendencies of mind are unusually strong) involves the discipline of the ascent of attention into the domain of the superconscious mind (or the Cosmic Mind) via the Ajna Door (especially in deep meditation). Some may be significantly attached (or otherwise moved) to the subtle possibilities of mind, so that they must practice (even for a significant period of time) in the domain of the superconscious mind (above attention to body and breath). Therefore, in order to quicken the course, distractions must be transcended. The discipline in the fifth stage of life in the Way of the Heart is, thus, based on the conservative discipline of the total mind, including the superconscious mind, just as the previous developmental stages of the practice of the Way of the Heart are based on the conservative discipline of food and breath and feeling. (And, in fact, all disciplines of the body-mind are, effectively, disciplines of attention, which is the functional core or root of the body-mind, and, therefore, in the Way of the Heart, all disciplines of the body-mind serve to Release attention, and feeling and energy as well, to the Great Process of listening, and then hearing, and then seeing, all in the context of Ishta-Guru-Bhakti Yoga.)

The ascending discipline of mind itself must be founded on the stable equanimity of the total body-mind (Realized via the disciplines of all the previous developmental stages of the practice of the Way of the Heart). The ascending discipline of mind is itself a matter of the full submission of attention into the Spirit-Current at the Ajna Door. This practice, done with great ease, and great attention above, allows attention to ascend through the progressively subtle levels of the higher or superconscious mind (or the superconscious Light above the gross body and the gross world).

The discipline of mind corresponds to the traditional Raja Yoga (which is based on, and thus includes, Karma Yoga, Bhakti Yoga, and Hatha Yoga). Raja Yoga (and all of its preliminary or otherwise generally associated Yogic disciplines) also traditionally (or potentially) includes Mantra Yoga and Japa Yoga (or the Devotional and progressively meditative use of Directly Blessed, Gifted, or Empowered Word-Signs, Divine Names, or Sat-Guru Names), Nada Yoga (or ascent via attention to subtle internal sounds), Kundalini Yoga (or ascent via the Spirit-Current and its Revealed Light or internally perceived lights), and Laya Yoga (or dissolution of the total mind and the resolution of attention in the Matrix of the Spirit-Current above the body-mind, in fifth stage conditional Nirvikalpa Samadhi). The progressive practice (or Yoga of "Consideration") of the Way of the Heart potentially includes all of these Yogas and all potential aspects of the Spiritual Process. Just so, it includes the stages of Jnana Yoga, which are beyond Raja Yoga.

The unconscious mind, the subconscious mind, and the conscious mind together form the manomayakosha. All of that is only the personal and lower conditional psyche, and it is typically expressed in association with breath, emotion, and the gross food body (or the gross senses) as the ordinary mind of the waking state. The ordinary mind also expresses itself in subtler forms, as in revery, or in dreams, but the mind may also express itself in extraordinary or higher forms, as in superconscious revery, or in Revelatory dreams and visions. When the subtler and higher mind is expressed in the form of superconscious visions and Revelations, attention has reached into the superconscious dimension of mind, beyond the gross body and its world. That superconscious field of mind is the outer field of vijnanamayakosha (which also includes the discriminative faculty of higher intelligence and the basic mental conception or assertion of the "I", or the will, of conditionally manifested being).

Practice of the Way of the Heart in the (potential) context of the fifth stage of life involves the ascent of attention via the discipline of mind (based on continued conservative discipline of the gross food body and the ascending discipline, or "conductivity", of breath and feeling in the Spirit-Current). That ascent may become the full elaboration of Raja Yoga (even to the degree of fifth stage conditional Nirvikalpa Samadhi). However, if mind is subjected to the fullest discipline of self-understanding, the contractions that appear as the forms of mind will (thereby, and most directly) lose their attractive capability, and the root of vijnanamayakosha (or the root of the total mind), which is attention itself, will become the "hitching post" of the Yoga of "Consideration".

X

The root-mind is not the subtle display of Universal (or Cosmic) mind and experience. The root-mind is self-contraction itself. Its root-form in the mind is egoity, or the "I" (or apparently separate consciousness) of the conditional self, which is, at its very root, simply, functional attention itself.

Traditional Jnana Yoga goes beyond the psychic ascent of Raja Yoga by means of Native Identification with the Witness-Consciousness, and, in some cases, by holding on to the "I"-thought, or, simply, the "I"-feeling, and by tracing it to its Source in the heart. Aham Sphurana, the Presence (or original Spirit-Current) That is (Prior to all thought) the Source of the original "I" (or self-contraction), is (or may, by Grace, be Revealed to be) in the heart, on the right side. By feeling-Contemplation of (and Native Identification with) the Native Feeling of Being (or Aham Sphurana), via (and Prior to) the "I"-feeling in the right side of the heart, the Process goes (by Grace) beyond the separate "I" to its Ultimate Source, Which is Consciousness Itself.

In the Way of the Heart, the sixth stage Process associated with Jnana Yoga is developed as a direct (or Grace-Given) extension of Ishta-Guru-Bhakti Yoga. That is to say, in formal meditation, either through self-Enquiry (in the form "Avoiding relationship?") and (or) non-verbal Re-cognition of gross, subtle, and causal forms of self-contraction, or through True Prayer (perhaps in the technically "elaborate" form of Mahamantra Meditation, or even in the technically "simplest" form of the Invocation of Me via My principal Name, "Da"), or through (technically "elaborate") Hridaya-Vichara (which I generally refer to as "Feeling-Enquiry"), the devotee transcends the self-contraction (even in its root-form, which is attention itself) and becomes Identified (by Grace) with What <u>Is</u> when the self-contraction is absent. (Even the technically "elaborate" sixth stage practice of Feeling-Enquiry is a form of Ishta-Guru-Bhakti Yoga, based on immediately previous <u>effective</u> practice of Ishta-Guru-Bhakti Yoga via the form of self-Enquiry and Re-cognition, or via the form of True Prayer.) Thus, in the Way of the Heart, the descending-ascending Process moves (or would move) into the context of the sixth stage of life, or the Heart-Domain of the Witness-Consciousness, the Aham Sphurana, and Consciousness Itself, via the Principle "you become What you meditate on (or Identify with)", and, in the Way of the Heart, the sixth stage Process fulfills itself in the spontaneous transition to the seventh stage Process via the Ultimate Principle "You Always Already Are What You Always Already <u>Are</u>".

Even before the final elaboration of fifth stage possibilities (in fifth stage conditional Nirvikalpa Samadhi), and even in the midst of practice in the context of the fourth stage of life (very likely, in the Way of the Heart, as early as the point of basic maturity in the first actually seeing stage of practice in the context of the "basic" fourth stage of life), attention can be Released from search or attachment relative to conditional objects (subtle or gross) and so become Free to Realize Native Identification with its own Source, Which <u>Is</u> Consciousness (Realized as the Witness of conditional objects, forms, states, and others). When attention relaxes and subsides in Consciousness <u>Itself</u>, the Spirit-Current resolves into the Sphurana (or the Native Love-Bliss-

Current, or Feeling of Being) in the right side of the heart. When the Perfect Status of Consciousness Itself becomes Obvious in this Process, there is the Realization of Consciousness in Itself (generally via Jnana Samadhi), and then Sahaj Samadhi (or Consciousness as the "Bright" Divine Self-Condition of all conditions). And Sahaj Samadhi, "Open Eyes", or Self-Abiding Divine Recognition of all phenomenal or conditional forms and states, may also be Realized directly, without necessarily being preceded by either fifth stage conditional Nirvikalpa Samadhi or Jnana Samadhi (which is sixth stage conditional Nirvikalpa Samadhi), although Jnana Samadhi is generally (in most cases) necessary (and, if it does not occur, its transitional function would necessarily be served by forms of profoundly deep, but not absolutely phenomena-excluding, meditation).

The Aham Sphurana, or Consciousness associated with the Inherent Radiance of the Spirit-Current in the right side of the heart, is the First Sign of the penetration and transcendence of the causal body, or anandamayakosha (the seat or heart of conditional bliss). The causal body is (apparently) conditionally associated with egoity (or separate Consciousness), in the form of an illusion that Consciousness is separate and un-Illumined in deep sleep. Truly, all illusions, being a part of mind, arise only with the mind, and, therefore, only when dreams and thoughts arise in the dreaming and waking states. Therefore, the illusion of separateness and non-Illumination associated with the causal body and deep sleep is, in general, only a presumption <u>about</u> the sleep state, and that presumption arises in the mind in the states of dreaming and waking. However, that presumption (or feeling) is perhaps also a characteristic of the sleep state itself, and, as such, it is an indication that the mind, as a primary self-contraction, is somehow still effective in its latent or dormant presence in the state of deep sleep.

In deep sleep, beyond the dreaming or waking experience of the body-mind, the Inherent or Native and Transcendental Self-Bliss (or Perfect Love-Bliss) is "touched" (because the body-mind has become relatively inactive, or latent, in Consciousness

Itself), but dreaming or waking states quickly arise from this latency, and then the self-contracting reaction to identification with the body-mind surrounds the heart (and Consciousness Itself) with more intense illusions that "loudly" suggest (while sleep perhaps only "whispers") that Consciousness is separate, limited, and conditional (rather than Transcendental, Divine, Inherent, or Self-Existing, and Inherently Spiritual, or Self-Radiant). Likewise, the causal tendency, or root-tendency, of self-contraction is associated with the automatic arising of attention toward mind and body (or subtle and gross conditions). Therefore, the root of the causal tendency is not originally and constantly expressed as the "I"-thought, but as attention itself (which is the simple, or thoughtless, feeling of relatedness, or the most primitive and formless feeling of contraction, or of "difference") in and of Consciousness Itself, associated with the "causal stress" (or conditional feeling-vibration) in the right side of the heart. And these appearances or illusions continue to veil the Very Being, until the causal knot is penetrated (or the depth of the Aham Sphurana is entered), and the Free Transcendental Divine Status of Consciousness Itself, Prior to the body-mind and the world, is Realized.

Sleep is not Transcendental Divine Self-Realization, nor is it the Way to It. The shapeless and deep causal presumption of separateness remains, and all the subtle and gross sheaths are also hidden (and merely, or nearly, "speechless") in mere sleep. Thus, dreaming and waking follow (or tend to follow) sleep, just as every kind of experience returns (or tends to return) after death.

Even the ego of sleep must be transcended in Consciousness Itself. Sleep is rest in the Inherent Love-Bliss of the Transcendental (and Inherently Spiritual) Divine Self, but with a most subtle contraction (of latent mind, or body-mind) into separateness, or non-Awakeness, or the apparent diminishment (or non-Awareness) of Freedom and Love-Bliss.

The causal knot (or "causal stress", the natural vibration inherently associated with conditional "I"-feeling, or the feeling of relatedness, and also naturally associated with the right side of the heart) is not fully penetrated (or transcended) in mere sleep, nor is the Aham Sphurana entered by sleep itself. The essence of mind persists, although latently, in deep sleep. Only equally (and more) persistent sadhana, or real and effective practice of the Way of the Heart, to the degree of Full Awakening to Consciousness Itself and spontaneous Divine Recognition of all conditional arising, Releases and Outshines the mind and all conditional or apparent forms.

The Transcendental (and Inherently Spiritual) Divine Self is "touched" in deep sleep, but It may likewise be "touched" in the dreaming and waking states, via meditation and the Process of Transcendental Awakening. Only persistence in the transcendence of attention, or of self-contraction, allows the direct and Inherently Perfect Realization of the Always Already Fully Awake and Transcendental (and Inherently Spiritual) Divine Self, or Consciousness Itself, beyond the physical body, beyond every level of the mind, beyond thought, beyond images in mind, beyond attention, beyond self-contraction, beyond reaction, beyond action, beyond avoidance, separation, separateness, independence, separativeness, "difference", relatedness, limitation, dis-ease, illusion, dependence, threat, fear, pain, conditional pleasure, others, objects, places, time, desire, attachment, conditional love, sorrow, anger, death, futility, and the apparent diminishment (or even non-Awareness) of Freedom and Love-Bliss.

When the self-contraction (in its root-form, which is attention) is transcended in the Realization of Native or Inherent Identification with Consciousness Itself (Prior to the body-mind), the Truth of Consciousness Itself becomes Inherently Obvious. And, thereafter, even if conditions apparently arise (whether in the waking, the dreaming, or the sleeping state), they are Inherently Recognizable as transparent, or merely apparent, and non-binding modifications of the Divine Self-Radiance of Self-Existing Consciousness Itself.

XI

The Process of the Yoga of "Consideration" in the context of the fourth stage of life (and thus in continuity with the first three stages of life) depends on maintenance of the feeling of identification with the gross body (or the gross body-mind itself, and its natural relations). When that feeling (which is self-contraction) is transcended in the Way of the Heart, practice moves (or may move) into the context of the fifth stage of life.

The Process of the Yoga of "Consideration" in the context of the fifth stage of life in the Way of the Heart depends on maintenance of the feeling of identification with the subtle body (or the conditional "I" itself, and the total mind, including all of its natural energies and relations). When that feeling (which is self-contraction) is transcended, practice of the Way of the Heart moves into the context of the sixth stage of life.

The Process of the Yoga of "Consideration" in the context of the sixth stage of life in the Way of the Heart relates to (and thus "Considers") the feeling of identification with the causal body (or the feeling of relatedness itself, which is the essence of attention itself) and the associated (or resultant) feeling that Consciousness (as the Witness of conditions) is perhaps separate, limited, and conditional. When, in the Way of the Heart, that complex of feeling (which is self-contraction) is transcended in the Simple (or Native) Feeling of Being (or the Aham Sphurana) and, then, in the Inherent Realization of the "Bright" Transcendental Divine Self-Condition of Consciousness Itself, practice in the Way of the Heart moves through the sixth stage of life and into the context of the seventh stage of life.

Truly, in the Way of the Heart, all of these stages of the transcendence of self-contraction (leading to the Native Realization of Consciousness Itself, spontaneously, or Always Already, and Divinely, Recognizing whatever apparently arises) may, by Grace, be Quickened (and, thus, most directly gone beyond). It is only necessary to listen to Me, and to hear Me, and to see Me.

96

To hear Me is (first) to "consider" (or truly listen to) My Arguments (and My Revealed Person), until (or to the degree that) you thoroughly observe and most fundamentally understand and are truly Released of the motive of self-contraction (and made capable to directly transcend it). Ultimately, it is simply (by Grace) to <u>Be</u>, Identical to the Original Heart-Current or Native Feeling of Being, Inherently Free of identification with the body-mind and attention (or the feeling of relatedness, otherness, separateness, "difference", and contraction). To hear Me Perfectly is to Stand in Native Identification with Consciousness Itself.

To see Me is to be truly heart-attracted in your attention to Me as Ishta. To submit to such heart-attractedness is to be drawn beyond all of the layers of conditional or contracted self-identity and conditional or contracted self-experience. To see Me Perfectly is to be Awakened, beyond the gesture of self-contraction, to the Transcendental (and Inherently Spiritual) Divine Self-Condition In Which and As Which I always Stand before you, within you, and <u>As</u> You.

If you will allow listening, and then hearing, and then seeing to be Awakened and magnified, and if you will express each and all of them through real conservative discipline of the body-mind and real Devotional discipline of attention, then Inherently Perfect Awakening to the seventh stage "practice"[17] (or Divinely Enlightened Demonstration) of the Way of the Heart can certainly be Realized (ultimately), by Grace.

---

17. Heart-Master Da Love-Ananda's use of the quotation marks around the term "practice" indicates the paradoxical meaning of this word when applied to His Divine Self-Realization and to the Divine Self-Realization of all practitioners of the Way of the Heart. In the seventh, or Divinely Self-Realized, stage of life in the Way of the Heart, the psycho-physical expression of that Realization is, so to speak, a "practice" only in the sense of simple action. It is not, in contrast to the stages previous to the seventh stage, a discipline intended to counter egoic tendencies that would otherwise dominate body and mind.

XII

The simple (or thoughtless) <u>feeling</u> of relatedness is the essence of attention, and it is the original or first form of self-contraction. Paradoxically, the feeling of relatedness is the very essence of "Narcissus", the self-contraction, or the avoidance of relationship. Therefore, in the Way of the Heart, this "feeling" of relatedness is to be discovered, and then transcended.

The Way of the Heart develops through listening to My Arguments (and to My Person). Such listening becomes thorough self-observation, and then most fundamental self-understanding (or true hearing). Then hearing becomes seeing, or Spiritual Regeneration, via the Process of Spirit-Baptism (which is Regeneration and Magnification of the Divine Spirit-Current, by Grace, and Awakening of the fullest Devotional, and directly Spiritual, Acknowledgement of Me as Ishta, or the Form and Presence and State of the Spiritual and Transcendental Divine Person or Reality).

The real Spiritual practice (or true Spiritual discipline) of the Way of the Heart develops only on the basis of attentive listening, true hearing, and clear seeing. On that basis, the real Spiritual practice may, in the case of some seeing devotees (in the Devotional Way of Insight, as practiced in the Way of the Heart), be continued in the form of self-Enquiry (in the form "Avoiding relationship?"), and then persistent non-verbal Re-cognition (or direct transcendence) of every form of self-contraction (gross, subtle, and causal), until Consciousness Itself is Revealed as the Obvious Truth.

That same listening and hearing and seeing and real Spiritual practicing may, in the case of other seeing devotees (in the Devotional Way of Faith, as practiced in the Way of the Heart), continue (and develop further) in the form of the Process of True Prayer, or of instant self-surrender (and progressive self-transcendence) via (Spiritually) Devotional Communion with Me (and, Thus and Thereby, with the Divine Person). And, in the technically "fully elaborated" practice of the Way of the Heart, such <u>Spiritual</u> Communion (via True Prayer) is Realized (by Grace) first (at practicing stage two) via the "Easy Prayer" of Spiritual Invocation of Me, Spiritual feeling-Contemplation of Me, and Surrender to My Spiritual Grace, then (at practicing stage three) via the Prayer of Remembrance, and, finally (at practicing stage four, and beyond, even through practicing stage six), via Mahamantra Meditation.

In the Way of the Heart, Mahamantra Meditation is meditation via Spiritually Potentized Word-Signs (Given by Me, and engaged silently, with the "tongue of the mind"). The basic (principal, or original) Mahamantra I have Given is "Om Ma Da".[18] However, My devotee (practicing the Devotional Way of

18. In the Way of the Heart, the Word-Sign "Om" indicates the Native Feeling of Being, or the Transcendental, and Inherently Spiritual, Divine Condition, the Self of all beings. It Invokes the Self-Father, Who is in the "Husband Position" in relation to conditional forms and events. Traditionally, "Om" (also transliterated "Aum"), is the most comprehensive and venerable symbol of Spiritual knowledge in Hinduism. The Mantra "Om" was first described in the Upanishads, and it is regarded by some to be the basis or seed of all mantras. It is the root syllable of origination and dissolution. Thus, "Om" is understood to be a direct expression of the Spiritual Power of the Divine or Absolute Being, from which all existence proceeds.

The Mantra "Ma" and its variants "Sri" and "Hrim", which are mentioned below, designate the Mother-Force, Shakti-Force, or Goddess-Power, or the Spiritual Radiance of the Divine Self. "Ma" means "Divine Mother", revered in many traditions as the Creatress and Origin of the universe, as well as the primordial Energy of existence, which is never changed or reduced in any way. The historical reference to the goddess "Sri" first appeared in the Vedas, where she was described as the personification of prosperity or luck, later associated with Lakshmi, the post-Vedic goddess of fortune and beauty. Often "Sri" is used as another Name for Lakshmi herself. "Hrim" is one of the primal "mula" ("root") or "bija" ("seed") mantras used in the esoteric Yoga of sound, Mantra Yoga. It is also associated with the Goddess-Power that presides over all conditional worlds.

Traditionally, the Goddess-Power designated by the Mantras "Ma", "Sri", and "Hrim" is viewed, by itself, as the source of "Maya" or the deluding power of conditional existence. However, when Husbanded by the Self-Father, as Sri Da Avabhasa has Revealed, this Great Power is associated with Enlightenment, or the lifting of the veil of illusion.

The Name "Da" points to the Giver of Divine Grace. It is an ancient Name of the Divine Person, in Whom the Self-Father and Mother-Power are One. "Da" is the One Who Gives Liberation Itself.

Revered in many sacred esoteric traditions, the syllable or sound "Da" means "the One Who Gives". The Tibetan Buddhists regard the syllable "Da" as most auspicious, and they assign numerous holy meanings to it: "Da" symbolizes a gift; it is "the Entrance to all Dharma" (that is, the Source of all knowledge); and it is a symbol of That Which is "deprived of nothing [and] takes away nothing, hence it sets free everything, i.e., gives salvation". In Sanskrit, "Da" means principally "to give or to bestow", but also "to destroy", and it is connected as well with the God Vishnu, the "Sustainer". Thus, "Da" is anciently aligned to all three of the principal Divine Beings, Forces, or Attributes in the Hindu tradition, Brahma (the Creator, Generator, or Giver), Vishnu (the Sustainer), and Siva (the Destroyer).

Faith) may (at the beginning of practicing stage four of the technically "fully elaborated" form of the Way of the Heart) choose any one of several forms of the Mahamantra for use in Mahamantra Meditation. Either "Om Hrim Da" or "Om Sri Da", which are variant forms of "Om Ma Da", may be used as an alternative to "Om Ma Da". Also, the chosen form of the Mahamantra (and the particular form of the practice of Mahamantra Meditation itself) may, in the case of some devotees, correspond to the traditional form and practice of either the Guru Mantra or Ajapa-Japa (in the general manner of So-Ham Japa[19]).

My devotees (practicing the Devotional Way of Faith) may (beginning at practicing stage four, in the technically "fully elaborated" form of the Way of the Heart) use the traditional description of the Guru Mantra as a working model for their own practice of Mahamantra Meditation (in the manner of the Guru Mantra) in the feeling-Contemplation of My bodily (human) Form, and My Spiritual (and Always Blessing) Pres-

19. The traditional Guru Mantra is "Guru Om". It is used in the manner of meditative prayer to maintain one's loving Remembrance of or devotional connection to the Guru, whose Transmission of Blessing quickens the practice of devotees and Awakens Realization in them. Those devotees of Sri Da Avabhasa who engage this practice use His Names (according to His particular Instructions), rather than the traditional Mantra ("Guru Om").

"Japa" is a Sanskrit term for the practice of devotion to the Divine (often, in the Form of the Guru) via prayerful recitation of a mantra, often composed of one or more Divine (or Divinely Manifested) Names. "Ajapa-Japa", which means literally "the recitation that goes beyond recitation", signifies the use of a mantra linked to the natural breath-cycle, or the intake and release of psychic (or psychoactive) energy (or "prana", also known as "hamsa", or "hansa"). Yogis who observe this psychic process in themselves, particularly as it occurs in meditation, hear the natural mantra of the breath as "So-Ham" (or, in reverse, "Ham-Sa"). Thus, there is a symbolic connection between the breath, as "hamsa", and the Transcendental Self, as "Paramahamsa" (also spelled "Paramahansa"). In the advanced practice of Ajapa-Japa, the being is released from identification with the bodily mechanism of the breath (and from identification with the body-mind altogether) by Identification with the Matrix of the Free Spirit-Current (which is above the body-mind) and, ultimately, the Transcendental Self (which is utterly prior to the body-mind and the self-contraction of attention).

The So-Ham mantra is composed of the Sanskrit words "So" (from "Sah", meaning "He", and signifying God and Guru) and "Ham" (from "Aham", meaning "I", or "I Am"). Thus, "So-Ham", ("So ham", or "Sah-Aham") means "I Am He", indicating Spiritual Identity with the Transcendental Divine Self, Realized through the Graceful Help of the Guru. Both Rudi and Swami Muktananda recommended the practice of So-Ham Japa to their devotees, although, beyond a relatively brief period of intensive experimentation with So-Ham Japa, Sri Da Avabhasa did not choose to assume this particular discipline in the years of His own practice.

ence, and My Very (and Inherently Perfect) State.[20] In the Way of the Heart, the devotee who would practice Mahamantra Meditation in the traditional manner of the Guru Mantra is Called to Embrace and to be Embraced by Me (and, Thus and Thereby, to Embrace and to be Embraced by the Divine Person), either via the Mahamantra in the form "Da Avabhasa Om", or via the Mahamantra in the form "Da Love-Ananda Om",[21] or via the Mahamantra in the form "Da-Guru Om", or via the Mahamantra in the form "Da Om". (When engaged in the likeness or in the manner of the traditional Guru Mantra,

20. The traditional practice of the Guru Mantra is summarized and described in *Play of Consciousness (Chitshakti Vilas),* by Swami Muktananda. In *Chitshakti Vilas* Swami Muktananda makes clear that, in essence, to practice the Guru Mantra is to meditate on the Guru as All-Pervading Energy and Consciousness, becoming absorbed in the Guru to the point that one loses oneself in the Guru and the Guru does the meditation.

The following moving passage describes Swami Muktananda's meditative absorption in his Guru, Swami Nityananda:

As I meditated, my mind became steady. I meditated with the awareness that the whole outside world was completely filled with him. The few thoughts that remained, I directed inward to the contemplation of Nityananda. First of all, I touched my head, thinking of Nityananda. Nityananda in my head, Nityananda in my skull, my dear Nityananda in my ears, Nityananda in the light of my eyes, Sri Guru Nityananda in my throat, Nityananda in my shoulders, Nityananda in my hands, Baba Nityananda in my fingers, Nityananda the Self in my heart, Sri Nityananda in my stomach, Sri Nityananda the lord of yoga in my waist, Guru Nityananda in my thighs, Nityananda in my knees, Nityananda in my legs, Nityananda in my feet. In this way I installed him throughout my entire body. As I touched each part, I repeated, Guru Om, Guru Om, Guru Om, strengthening my meditation on Sri Bhagavan Nityananda. What joy! My heart lightened, its anguish and passion disappeared. Fresh and happy vibrations ran through me, and I was overcome by a rush of ecstasy. When you meditate on ecstatic beings, you become ecstatic yourself. . . .

And so I installed the Guru in every part of my body with deepest love and then became completely lost in worship. . . . I had been meditating for three hours, but so far had only finished half the meditation. I started to meditate from the feet upward. I touched my feet and said, O Guru, please be here. Nityananda in my feet, Nityananda in my knees. . . . In this way, I again meditated on my great Guru Nityananda from my toes to my head. (Play of Consciousness [Chitshakti Vilas] *[San Francisco: Harper & Row, 1978], pp. 60-61.)*

As Sri Da Avabhasa indicates in this section of His Essay, this description of the traditional practice of the Guru Mantra provides a good working model for the practice, in the Way of the Heart, of Mahamantra Meditation in the manner of the Guru Mantra. (Indeed, the approach to the Sat-Guru that characterizes the traditional practice of the Guru Mantra is the essence of Ishta-Guru-Bhakti Yoga.)

Beyond this, as with every other form of practice described in the literature of the Way of the Heart, the individual devotee must Realize the details of practice by practice itself (supported, guided, counseled, and personally instructed within the formal practicing orders of devotees of Sri Da Avabhasa).

21. In these variant forms of the Mahamantra, the Name "Avabhasa" means (in Sanskrit) "brightness", "appearance", "manifestation", "splendor", "lustre", "light", "knowledge", and the Name "Love-Ananda" simply means "Love-Bliss".

the Mahamantra always ends in, and thus leads toward, the Primal Monosyllable "Om", whereas the Mahamantra Given by Me in the form "Om Ma Da", and its variants, begins with, and, thus, proceeds from the Primal Monosyllable "Om". And, likewise, the two by Me Given variants of the Sat-Guru-Naama Mantra[22] begin with, and, thus, proceed from, the Primal Monosyllable "Om". In either case, whether the Mahamantra begins or ends with "Om", this Primal Monosyllable Indicates the Original, or Inherent and Ultimate, Spirit-Energy at the "point" of Origin, and at the "point" of Dissolution, of Mahamantra, mind, body, and all forms and, Ultimately, the Primal Monosyllable "Om" Indicates the Native Source, or the Self-Existing and Self-Radiant Transcendental, and Inherently Spiritual, Divine Self-Consciousness That Is the Always Already Free and Perfectly Subjective Source, or Source-Condition, of all appearances.)

Alternatively, My devotees (practicing the Devotional Way of Faith) who practice the technically "fully elaborated" form of the Way of the Heart (at practicing stages four, five, and even six) may practice Mahamantra Meditation in the general manner of the traditional So-Ham Japa.[23] However, such devotees who choose to practice Mahamantra Meditation in the <u>general</u>

22. Traditionally, the Divinely Self-Realized Adept Gives His disciples His own Name to use in prayer and meditation since, for human beings, the human Sat-Guru is the most potently transformative Form of the Divine Person. The two variants of the Sat-Guru-Naama Mantra, "Om Sri Da Avabhasa Hridayam" and "Om Sri Da Love-Ananda Hridayam", Given by Heart-Master Da, are two of the Mantras used by practitioners of the Way of the Heart.

Hridaya-Samartha Sat-Guru Da Love-Ananda has Written that the Names of the Sat-Guru (and thus the Names of the Divine Being) are "equivalents of God, ways of approximating the Deity, or the Transcendental Reality. They do not simply mean God, or the Blessing of God. They are the verbal or audible Form of the Divine." Since ancient times, the Empowered Name of one's Sat-Guru has been an auspicious focus for Contemplation of the Divine Person.

The Sat-Guru-Naama Mantra (in both of its variants) in the Way of the Heart is described in *The Dawn Horse Testament,* and, like all other forms of Name, Mantra, or Mahamantra Given by Heart-Master Da Love-Ananda to His devotees, it must be received via formal initiation at the appropriate stage of formal practice.

23. In the New Standard Edition of *The Knee of Listening,* Heart-Master Da describes the traditional practice of So-Ham Japa (a form of Ajapa-Japa), as He was instructed by Swami Muktananda, His Spiritual Teacher from 1968-1970. Also, in the book entitled *So ham Japa: A Meditation Technique for Everyone,* by Swami Muktananda Paramahansa, the traditional practice of So-Ham Japa is summarized and described.

manner of So-Ham Japa are Called to do Ajapa-Japa via the Mahamantra "Da-Om" (rather than "So-Ham"). In that case, "Da" is to be engaged silently (with "the tongue of the mind") on exhalation and "Om" (which is simply a shortened version, or Epitome, of "So-Ham") is to be engaged silently (with "the tongue of the mind") on inhalation. (Also, as an alternative to such engagement of the Mahamantra in the form "Da-Om", devotees in the Way of the Heart who practice Mahamantra Meditation in the general manner of So-Ham Japa, or Da-Om Japa, may practice simple feeling-observation of the "meaningless" natural sounds of exhalation and inhalation.)[24]

When Mahamantra Meditation is practiced in the form (or even in the general manner) of Da-Om Japa, even every breath Announces the Giver of Spirit-Life ("Da") and, Ultimately, the Ultimate Truth of the Way of the Heart ("The Perfectly Subjective Source of 'I' Is Da", or "Da Is the Inherent or Native Feeling of Being"). Therefore, the practice of this Da-Om Japa is not an effort of the conditional self (or the egoic body-mind) to Identify with Me (and, Thus and Thereby, with the Divine Person and Self-Condition). Rather, Inherent Identification with Me (and, Thus and Thereby, with the Divine Person and Self-Condition) is simply observed (and spontaneously Affirmed) with each breath (or in each moment of simple observation and feeling).

In the case of Da-Om Japa, the breath may simply be observed (and the Spirit-Current felt) at the Ajna Door (and above), with "Da" on exhalation and "Om" on inhalation. Alternatively, the breath and its own natural or "meaningless" sounds may simply be observed and felt (along with the Inherent Love-Bliss of the Spirit-Current) at the Ajna Door and

24. Traditionally So-Ham Japa is performed by coordinating the repetition of "So-Ham" with the breath. Swami Muktananda Taught the repetition of "So" on inhalation and "Ham" on exhalation.

Heart-Master Da Love-Ananda Recommends Ajapa-Japa in the form of Da-Om Japa, rather than the traditional So-Ham Japa. In Da-Om Japa, the Word-Sign "Da" is engaged on exhalation, and the Word Sign "Om" is engaged on inhalation.

The combination "Da-Om" signifies release of the self-contraction at the heart (or at the root of breath and heartbeat) and spontaneous or inherent Realization of Heart-Master Da Love-Ananda's Spiritual (and Always Blessing) Presence (and, ultimately, the Realization of Identification with His Very, and Inherently Perfect, State).

above. However, either of these forms of ascended concentration is usually to be preceded (and then periodically, or at least finally, followed) by a period of Da-Om Japa in which the breath, and the Spirit-Current Itself, are followed (and sometimes even deliberately engaged) in the pattern of the Circle. (In any case, Da-Om Japa, like any other by Me Given form of meditation in the Way of the Heart, is generally to be practiced while sitting in a relaxed, spinally erect posture. The tongue should rest, or even press, against the roof of the mouth, in order to maintain a frontal circuit between the head and the throat and trunk. The mouth should remain closed, and all breathing should be exercised via the nose.)

When Da-Om Japa is engaged in the pattern of the Circle (while feeling the Spirit-Current descend in the frontal line, to the bodily base), the Word-Sign "Da" (indicating My Mere and Blessing Presence, and, Thus and Thereby, the Mere and Blessing Presence of the Divine Person and Self-Condition) is to be engaged during (or with) every exhalation (or else the "meaningless" natural sound of the exhaled breath is to be attended to during every exhalation). As exhalation proceeds toward a full but easeful completion, the solar plexus and abdomen should be permitted to be drawn inwards and upwards, slowly and easily, and the bodily base should be tensed (or drawn up) at the end of the exhalation, but only to the degree necessary to "seal" the bodily base and to direct or "shoot" the Spirit-Current up and back, into the spinal line and toward the Ajna Door and above. With every inhalation (while silently engaging either the Word-Sign "Om" or the "meaningless" natural sound of the inhaled breath), the frontal line should first be filled (while the bodily base continues to be inwardly drawn upwards) and fully (but comfortably) pressed out (at the solar plexus and the abdomen), so that the contractions (or knots) of the frontal line relax and open, thus releasing the Spirit-Current to be conducted into the spinal line. As the abdominal pressure increases, the Spirit-Current should be pulled up and otherwise felt flowing upwards along the spinal line to the Ajna Door and above.[25]

In this practice of Da-Om Japa (whether by following the breath in the Circle or by simply observing the breath at the Ajna Door), spontaneous kumbhak (or retention of the breath, and thus also of the Spirit-Current and attention, at the Ajna Door and above) will (perhaps) eventually occur (for varying lengths of time), generally at the full point of inhalation (but perhaps even at the empty point of exhalation and "shooting"). Kumbhak may also be intentionally engaged at times, but briefly, and generally at the full point of ascended inhalation (or perhaps also at the empty point of "shooting" via exhalation).

The devotee who practices Mahamantra Meditation should (at practicing stage four of the technically "fully elaborated" form of the Way of the Heart) choose <u>one</u> form of the Mahamantra and thereafter engage it steadily in daily meditation, without switching to any other of the alternative forms of the Mahamantra (or of Mahamantra practice). Whichever one of the alternative forms of the Mahamantra such a seeing devotee chooses, and whichever one of the three basic types of practice of Mahamantra Meditation such a seeing devotee engages (either the one that corresponds to My own unique description of Mahamantra Meditation,[26] or the one that corresponds to the

25. The technical exercise of lung-breathing Spirit-"conductivity" described by Heart-Master Da Avabhasa in this paragraph bears some likeness to the traditional exercise variously known as "bellows breathing", or "vase breathing", or simply "the vase" or "the pot-shape" in the Hindu, Buddhist, and Taoist Yogic traditions.

Traditionally, this practice is engaged in a deliberate search to attain specific phenomenal experiences, or modifications of the natural life-energy (or, optimally, of the Spirit-Current), for their own sake.

In the Way of the Heart, however, the only purpose of bellows breathing is as a supportive practice, which, via purification and release of obstructions in the Circle of the Spirit-Current, provides a stronger foundation for the senior practice of the "conscious process". It is not performed for its own sake or for the sake of the experiences it may produce.

Heart-Master Da Instructs His devotees that, in the Way of the Heart, bellows breathing is basically intended to be engaged only by practitioners in the "advanced" fourth stage of life and the fifth stage of life, although it may continue to be used (at random) in the sixth stage of life and the seventh stage of life by individuals who previously practiced in the ascending developmental stages of the Way of the Heart.

26. Please see *The Dawn Horse Testament* for Heart-Master Da Avabhasa's Instructions on the practice of Mahamantra Meditation.

traditional practice of the Guru Mantra, or the one that I call Da-Om Japa), the practice itself must (like <u>every</u> other by Me Given form of meditation practice engaged in the context of the "advanced" fourth stage of life, and the fifth stage of life, in the Way of the Heart) be profoundly <u>felt</u>, whole bodily, toward the crown of the head (and above, and beyond), and at or via the Ajna Door, but from the heart. Likewise, the practice must truly be self-transcending, and it must Realize <u>Divine</u> Communion (even without any Words in mind). In this manner, the practice of any by Me Given form of either True Prayer or self-Enquiry and Re-cognition eventually becomes Inherently Perfect Release of the self-contraction at the heart.

Whichever one of the by Me Given forms of meditation is practiced in the context of the "advanced" fourth stage of life, or the fifth stage of life, in the Way of the Heart, spontaneous kumbhak at the Ajna Door and above may occur at any moment of meditation. (And full spontaneous kumbhak, or suspension of breath, and fully upward suspension of attention from the downward passage to and below the brows, is the foundation event of fifth stage conditional Nirvikalpa Samadhi, which is the ultimate potential experiential fulfillment of the Yoga of ascent associated with the "advanced" fourth stage of life and the fifth stage of life in the Way of the Heart.) Likewise, during formal meditation practice in the context of the "advanced" fourth stage of life, or the fifth stage of life, in the Way of the Heart, attention should constantly be permitted to be drawn up in Love-Bliss via the Ajna Door, and all verbal activity of mind (even the silent verbal engagement of the Mahamantra, or My principal Name, "Da", or self-Enquiry) should be allowed to be progressively and then spontaneously replaced either by the feeling-Contemplation of the "touch" of the by Grace Revealed Spirit-Current (which is the immediate experience of Love-Bliss Itself) or by the simple observation (and release) of other subtle perceptions (primarily either subtle visions, or subtle lights, epitomized by the vision of the Cosmic Mandala, or subtle sounds, epitomized by a steady or uninterrupted hum or ring, which is the Carrier, or base sound, equivalent to the Word-Sign "Om" and to the "meaningless" natural sound of the inhaled or incoming breath). And even all subtle perceptions (as well as mental conceptions) should be thus persistently released toward the utterly silent and deeply objectless Love-Bliss-Illuminated Awareness above the brows (until all identification with the motives of attention, whether ascending or descending, is transcended in Free and Inherently Perfect Identification with the Witness-Consciousness, Which is the Sign of Self-Existing and Self-Radiant Divine Consciousness Itself).[27]

In all the advanced and the ultimate stages of the Way of the Heart (whether via the Process of self-Enquiry and Re-cognition, or via the Process of any by Me Given form of True Prayer, or via the Process of Feeling-Enquiry), attention is <u>dissolved</u> (or otherwise resolved). Every advanced Process (in the context of either the "basic" or the "advanced" fourth stage of life, and in the context of the fifth stage of life) in the Way of the Heart dissolves attention in My Spirit-Presence (even via the Circle of the body-mind). In the sixth stage (or first ultimate stage) of the Way of the Heart, attention is (by Grace) resolved in the Witness-Consciousness, then in the Aham Sphurana (or the Current of Love-Bliss associated with the right side of the heart), and, finally, in Consciousness Itself, Realized as the Inherent or Native Feeling of Being (Itself). And in the seventh stage (or most ultimate stage) of the Way of the Heart, attention is Always Already (and Divinely) Recognized (and thus transcended) in Consciousness Itself (Realized as the Feeling of Being, Itself).

In the context of the sixth stage of life in the Way of the Heart, the Great (and always "Radical", or most direct) Process of listening, hearing, seeing, and real practicing has developed into the "Perfect Practice" of the Way of the Heart. There are several alternative forms of practice in the context of the sixth stage of life in the Way of the Heart, but they are all very similar (and basically equivalent) to one another, and all correspond to what I call the "'Perfect Practice'" of the Way of the

27. All the technicalities to which Sri Da Avabhasa refers in this paragraph are fully described by Him in *The Dawn Horse Testament*.

Heart. These sixth stage practices (in the Way and Manner of the Heart) are associated with either self-Enquiry (and Re-cognition) or True Prayer or Feeling-Enquiry.[28]

If, in the sixth stage of life in the Way of the Heart, either self-Enquiry (and Re-cognition) or any (either technically "elaborate" or technically "simpler", or even technically "simplest") form of True Prayer is to be continued (including any form of True Prayer described, or otherwise referred to, in this essay), it is to be adapted to the sixth stage orientation and Manner of the "Perfect Practice". Also, as an alternative to (and, in the context of daily living, in random alternation with) either self-Enquiry (and Re-cognition) or True Prayer, the sixth stage discipline (and formal meditation practice) of (technically "elaborate") Feeling-Enquiry may (and, in some cases, must necessarily) be practiced, once practice of the Way of the Heart begins in the context of the sixth stage of life.

Therefore, those who are truly prepared to practice the Way of the Heart in the context of the sixth stage of life may (as appropriate) embrace any of the sixth stage practices I have indicated. All of these variations on the "Perfect Practice" of the Way of the Heart Realize Consciousness Itself (as God, Truth, or Reality) via <u>direct</u> and <u>immediate</u> Feeling-Identification with the (by Grace Revealed) Inherent Feeling of Being.

Whether through the sixth stage developments of self-Enquiry (and Re-cognition), or through the sixth stage fulfillment of True Prayer, or through Feeling-Enquiry, it is the self-contraction that is (in the Way of the Heart) to be observed, understood, and transcended. And the essential form, or first form, of self-contraction is attention itself, which is, in itself,

---

28. In this passage, Sri Da Avabhasa enumerates the practices that may be Given to practitioners in the sixth stage of life in the Way of the Heart. For a full explanation of the qualifications (and previous experience of the "conscious process") required for each practice, see *The Dawn Horse Testament*, chapter 43. *The Dawn Horse Testament* also describes how the various forms of the "conscious process" practiced previous to the sixth stage of life in the Way of the Heart are adapted to the "Perfect Practice".

All forms of the "Perfect Practice" are based on "considerations" Sri Da Avabhasa first elaborated in *The Knee of Listening* and *The Liberator (Eleutherios)*. His Instructions on Feeling-Enquiry are Given in detail in *The Lion Sutra*.

simply the feeling of relatedness.

And Priorly Awakened "practice", or Divinely Enlightened Demonstration in the context and manner of the seventh stage of life in the Way of the Heart, is only for those who have qualified for and then fulfilled the discipline of the Way of the Heart in the context of the sixth stage of life, and who have <u>thus</u> (by Grace) Realized the Transcendental (and Inherently Spiritual) Divine Self-Condition of attention, and of the feeling of relatedness, and of all conditional states of existence.

XIII

Mind is invocation.
Mind invokes (or calls forth) conditional experience and conditional knowledge, high and low.
Mind invokes apparent modification (and apparent modifications) of What Merely (or Inherently) <u>Is</u>.

Mind is the agent of self-contraction, and conditional experience and conditional knowledge are the results of mind.

Mind is itself the act of invocation, or the search for modifications, and it evolves only from self-contraction itself.

Therefore, the transcendence of mind is the transcendence of self-contraction, egoic invocation (or seeking), conditional experience, conditional knowledge, and all apparent modification of What <u>Is</u>. And such transcendence is the Way of the Heart.

Both the Process of self-Enquiry (and, eventually, Re-cognition) and the Process of True Prayer (including, in any moment or developmental stage of any by Me Given form of the practice of the Way of the Heart, the self-surrendering, self-forgetting, and self-transcending Invocation of Me by My principal Name, "Da") address and release (or feel beyond) contractions of the body-mind, but the body-mind itself (and, in the case of seeing devotees, the Spirit-Current in the context of the body-mind) is the conditionally (or naturally) presumed point of view of either Process, until practice begins in the context of the sixth stage of life (and thus from the "Point Of View" of the Witness-Consciousness).

The Process of Feeling-Enquiry also addresses and releases (or feels beyond) contractions of the body-mind, but the "Point Of View" of the Process is the Witness-Consciousness.

Even the Process of Self-Abiding Divine Recognition apparently addresses and releases (or feels beyond) contractions of the body-mind, but the "Point Of View" of that Great Process is the Always Already Given and Inherently Realized Position of Consciousness Itself, Which Is Self-Existing and Self-Radiant (or Inherently "Bright") Transcendental Divine Being.

Therefore, the Divinely Perfect (or seventh stage) Process of the Way of the Heart does not address or release or feel beyond contractions of the body-mind by first assuming (or presuming) either the point of view of the body-mind itself or the Witnessing "Point Of View" of the Witness-Consciousness. Rather, the Divinely Perfect (or seventh stage) Process of the Way of the Heart indeed addresses and releases (or feels beyond) whatever arises apparently (or conditionally), but whatever apparently arises is Inherently (and Divinely) Recognized (and Inherently Transcended) as a transparent (or merely apparent) and non-binding modification of Self-Existing and Self-Radiant Consciousness Itself. And such Divine Recognition can take place only Within and As the "Point Of View" That Is Consciousness Itself.

Transcendental Divine Recognition is the same as Transcendental Divine Self-Abiding (or Abiding As What Is Inherently, Always Already Prior to self-contraction or apparent modification). To Divinely Recognize what apparently arises is simply, or Merely, to Be (or to Self-Exist As) Self-Radiant Consciousness Itself, or the Inherent Love-Bliss of Being Itself (Which Is the "Bright", or Happiness Itself).

Either via the practice of self-Enquiry and Re-cognition, or via the practice of any by Me Given form of True Prayer, or via the practice of Feeling-Enquiry, specific contractions of the

110

body-mind are released (or felt beyond). Thus, in every moment of real self-Enquiry, or Re-cognition, or True Prayer, or Feeling-Enquiry, attention to self-contraction (even in the form of numberless psycho-physical objects and states) is replaced (or effectively transcended) by attention to (or feeling of) the fundamental (or unqualified, or objectless) feeling of relatedness. And when this feeling is itself really, truly, and stably Re-cognized (or otherwise released or felt beyond), Self-Existing and Self-Radiant Consciousness Itself is Revealed to Be That Which Is Always Already The Case (Prior to all self-contraction, or all apparent modification of Itself).

Self-Existing and Self-Radiant (or Inherently Love-Blissful) Consciousness Itself Is What Is (or Who Is). Conditional arising, self-contraction, or apparent modification (or conditioning) of Inherent Love-Bliss is an Illusion. Therefore, such arising is, in itself, Deluding (or an apparent Cause of Non-Recognition of whatever is apparently arising). Once such Non-Recognition, or Delusion, or Suffering of an Illusion, apparently arises, an apparent Struggle (or Spiritual Ordeal) becomes necessary, if Illusion, Delusion, or Non-Recognition is to be observed, understood, and transcended. Such is the Way of the Heart, until (by Grace) that Way is Utterly Awakened (or Natively Established) in Self-Existing and Self-Radiant Consciousness Itself (Inherently Most Prior to the body-mind itself, and Inherently Most Prior even to the Witness-Function of Consciousness). After that Graceful Awakening (which Initiates the seventh stage of life), the Way of the Heart is Realized to be Inherent (or Natively Self-Abiding, and Divine) Recognition of whatever apparently arises, including the feeling of relatedness (itself), or (Ultimately, or Most Simply) the feeling of "difference" (itself), which is the primitive essence of all that (apparently) arises.

XIV

The feeling of relatedness spontaneously and constantly communicates itself as the complex feeling of "difference" (or of not-Same and not-One) and separateness (or of dark and deprived independence of being, or aloneness, and craving for an "other") and limitation (or of small and threatened and inadequate being) and emptiness (or of non-Fullness, un-Happy futility of being, and the craving for any "thing" that fills). The feeling of relatedness (or any instant of attention) is self-contraction itself, at its original or causal level. And when I am Perfectly heard (by Perfect listening) and also Perfectly seen, the Process of real practice becomes the discipline of immediate and direct transcendence of attention itself (specifically via transcendence of this conditional feeling of relatedness) in the Inherent and Perfectly Subjective Spiritual, Transcendental, and Divine Feeling of Being (the Aham Sphurana, or the Spirit-Current in the right side of the heart). And this Process fulfills itself in Perfect Awakening to the "Bright" Spiritual, Transcendental, Divine, and Inherent Condition That Is Consciousness Itself, spontaneously and Divinely Recognizing whatever apparently arises (as a condition related to Consciousness) to Be Only Consciousness Itself, Inherent or Self-Existing Being Itself, or Inherent and Self-Radiant Love-Bliss Itself.

Indeed, if you will listen to Me and hear Me and see Me (each Perfectly) at the heart, you will (by Grace, and as and when Grace will have it) be established in (and As) the Witness-Consciousness, and the essence of self-contraction will be noticed (as the mindless, or thoughtless, imageless, speechless, and soundless feeling of relatedness, at the right side of the heart). When this establishment (in and As the Witness-Consciousness) and this noticing (of the feeling of relatedness, in the right side of the heart) become steady and profound, real practice will have spontaneously moved beyond all the distractions of attention in the others and objects and places and experiences and apparent knowledge associated with the first five stages of life. In this manner, practice of the Way of the Heart will be established in the context of the sixth stage of life. In the maturity of that transition, the unique discipline of attention (whereby attention itself is transcended) will be the immediate, always present, and persistent feeling (and Mere Witnessing) of the feeling of relatedness (in the right side of the heart), and the (subsequent) direct transcendence of the feeling of relatedness (in the Inherent Feeling of Being, Which Stands in and Prior to the right side of the Heart) by persisting in Merely Witnessing, and by feeling more and more deeply into and As That Which Is (and Is Itself Perfectly Prior to) the Witness-Consciousness Itself. And the Re-cognition, or otherwise steady inspection and direct transcendence, of the feeling of relatedness (in its Source, Which is the Inherent Feeling of Being, or Self-Radiant and Self-Existing Consciousness Itself) soon becomes Jnana Samadhi, or even Sahaj Samadhi (fully Awake As Awakeness Itself, even in the context of appearances).

Therefore, "consider" this: You are active as self-contraction. Indeed, you, as a conditional or psycho-physical personality or "I", are the activity of self-contraction.

The activity of self-contraction is suffering, it is deluding, and it is itself an illusion, or an illusory disease.

The activity of self-contraction is un-Necessary. The activity of self-contraction is not Ultimately Real (or Necessary), but it is only (apparently) being added to Reality. The activity of self-contraction is being superimposed on What Always Already Is.

The activity of self-contraction is dramatized in the gross bodily plane of experience as the complex avoidance of relationship. It is dramatized in the subtle plane of experience as emotions and thoughts. It is dramatized essentially (or at the original or causal level) as attention itself. And the essence of attention itself (in itself) is the root-feeling of relatedness. Observe all of this.

"I", or egoity, or self-contraction, or attention itself, is simply and originally the feeling of relatedness. The cognition of

"I", or relatedness, is self-contraction. The noticing of relatedness (or of any object) is self-contraction (or separation) and
the noticing of "difference". The transcendence of "I" (or of
self-contraction) is not the avoidance of relationship, but it is
the transcendence of relatedness, or of separateness, or of self-
contraction.

Therefore, transcend the separate and separative "I". Transcend self-contraction, Ultimately and Finally, by transcending it
directly, at its root. Transcend egoity, or self-contraction, or
attention itself, at its essential root, as the feeling of relatedness,
even before it becomes the object-seeking activity of attention.

If you listen to Me and hear Me and see Me to this Inherently Perfect degree, then meditate thus: "Locate" the Source of
self-contraction via the feeling of relatedness. Do this moment
to moment, in formal meditation. Constantly "Locate" (or Re-
"Locate") the feeling of relatedness. Do this via Feeling-Enquiry,
or self-Enquiry, or non-verbal Re-cognition, or one or another
version of True Prayer. Whichever form of this practice you
choose (or are otherwise obliged to choose, by virtue of the
form of practice that immediately preceded this transition),
"Locate" (thereby) the simple feeling of relatedness, and (by
Merely Witnessing the feeling of relatedness, and by Feeling As
What Is Prior to the feeling of relatedness) Stand Free at the
Source of the feeling of relatedness. The Source Is Freedom
Itself. Therefore, Realization of the Source is Realization of
Freedom Itself.

The Source that is (by Grace) to be "Located" and Realized
is not an Objective Source. No object of attention, however
Great, is the Ultimate Source of attention. The Source of the
feeling of relatedness is not any relation of that feeling (or any
relation or object or activity of attention), but It is That Which
Simply (or Always Already) Is, or That Which Is Obvious when
the feeling of relatedness (or attention, or self-contraction, or
the tacit feeling of "difference") is absent (or directly transcended). Therefore, the Immediate and Ultimate Source of the feeling of relatedness is Perfectly Subjective (or the Ultimate, Most

Prior, and Inherently Perfect Subject of the feeling of related-ness, rather than an objective relation of it, or even a Great Object of it). The Immediate and Ultimate Source of the feeling of relatedness (and, therefore, of self-contraction, or attention itself, or the tacit feeling of "difference") is Itself the Subject (or Very Self, or Consciousness) of that feeling. The Immediate and Ultimate Source of the feeling of relatedness is the Transcen-dental Subject, or Consciousness Itself, To Whom and In Whom and As Whom the "feeling" is arising.

The Ultimate (or Perfectly Subjective) Source of whatever is gross (or physical) or subtle (or emotional or mental) or causal (or egoic) Is What Is, Always and Already, when or if the feel-ing of relatedness does not arise (or even if it does arise).

What Is Is That Which Is when or if self-contraction is not added to What Is. What Is (or That Which Is) is not Finally or Ultimately Realized by the motion of attention toward any object (whether it is a lesser object or even a Great Object). This is because attention is itself a form (even the original form) of self-contraction itself.

Realization of Reality is Realization of What Is Prior to self-contraction. Therefore, It cannot be Realized by attention to any object, other, or place (however Great). It can only be Realized As It Is (or As That Which Obviously Is when there is no self-contraction). It Is That Which Is Obvious when the tacit feeling of relatedness (or the tacit feeling of "difference") is Released, or is simply not noticed, and is thus transcended.

"Consider" this (and Perfectly): What Is Behind the feeling of relatedness? What Is Perfectly (or Most Priorly) Subjective to the feeling of relatedness? What Is Always Already Standing, Most Prior, Even In the Very Place of the feeling of relatedness? "Locate" That (and Perfectly).

Perfectly Feel, "Locate", and Stand As the Source of the thoughtless, imageless, and silent heart-feeling of relatedness. Be That Source. Abide As That, even Divinely Recognizing (As That) whatever arises apparently or conditionally.

This meditation (or "consideration") is not a matter of

"Locating" any object, other, state, or place that stands (objectively) in front of attention, or (objectively) in front of the feeling of relatedness. It is a matter of "Locating" What Is There (In or At the Place of attention), Which Is the Source of attention, and Which <u>Is</u>, Prior to attention itself. What Is Always Already Standing There, when attention (or the feeling of relatedness) does not arise to the notice? It Is the Inherent (and Perfectly Subjective) Feeling of Being, or Consciousness Itself. Therefore, when it is Inherently Perfectly observed and understood that the feeling of relatedness (which is the root-essence of the body-mind and attention) is only self-contraction (and even the first form or root-form of all the gross, subtle, and causal forms of self-contraction), then let the feeling of relatedness be liberally Released in the Inherent Feeling (or Great Heart-Feeling) of Being.

By Grace, Perfectly deep inspection (or Inherently Perfect Witnessing) of the feeling of relatedness dissolves (or re-solves) the feeling of relatedness in the Inherent (or Most Prior) Feeling of Being, or the Great Heart-Feeling In Which it is arising. In that Event, only the Inherent Happiness of Consciousness Itself Stands Free and Still As the Obvious Reality. Thus, It Becomes Obvious: There <u>Is</u> Only Consciousness Itself, and Consciousness Itself Is God, Reality, Truth, and Happiness. Therefore, Realization of Consciousness Itself Is Realization of God, Reality, Truth, and Happiness!

XV

"C"onsider" this: The "I" of separate self is the body-mind. The body-mind is a product of Cosmic elemental forces. The body-mind is constantly dependent on those forces, and yet it is separated from them by its own independence or individuality. Consequently, the body-mind is constantly related to (and yet contracted from) the same elemental forces of which it is itself made, and of which all other forms or products of elemental forces are made. Indeed, the body-mind is always related to and yet separated from (or in tension with) all elemental (or Cosmic) forces and their forms or products. The self-contracted body-mind is itself the ego-"I", or attention, or self-contraction itself, or the tacit feeling of relatedness, or the tacit feeling of "difference".

Because this is so, the Perfectly mature practitioner of the Way of the Heart should constantly return to (or Always Already Abide At) the Place Where he or she Stands. That is to say, one should constantly return from the field in which one wanders, or, better still, there should be no wandering. (And attention is the wanderer, expressed as the body-mind, or will and desire, in relation to all kinds of Cosmic, or elemental, objects, relations, and states.)

The Perfectly mature practitioner of the Way of the Heart should constantly allow attention (and its objects, including every aspect of the body-mind) to subside, or be at rest, in the bodiless and mindless, or thoughtless, imageless, speechless, soundless, and heart-silent, <u>feeling</u> of relatedness.

If this <u>feeling</u> of relatedness is (itself) simply or merely and steadily inspected (or Witnessed), both the feeling (itself) and the inspection (or Witnessing) will dissolve spontaneously (like a mirage of water, when it is approached and inspected). In that instant of dissolution, the "pond of Narcissus" disappears (with its illusions of separate self), and What Remains Is the "Gaze" in the Heart, or the Feeling of Being (Itself), or the Self-Existing and Self-Radiant Form That <u>Is</u> Consciousness Itself.

Therefore, merely to steadily inspect (or merely to Witness, and, thus, to dissolve or directly transcend, and even cease to notice) the feeling of relatedness is Merely to <u>Be</u>, Free of the arising of attention in and to the forms and relations of mind and body. This is because the feeling of relatedness is itself the contraction that precedes (or is the essence and the background of) attention, mind, body, and their objects or relations.

To steadily inspect (or to Perfectly Witness) the feeling of relatedness (and, spontaneously, to Feel and Be the Condition That <u>Is</u> Prior to it) is to Stand (or Be) Where neither attention, nor mind, nor body, nor any objects, others, places, or conditional states arise.

Therefore, do not seek any object of attention. Do not seek. Do not casually wander as attention, or via attention. Do not identify with attention, for it is the self-contraction itself, and it is inherently and always moved toward objects, others, and conditional states.

To Release attention (or Be, Released from it) it is only necessary to Stand Prior to it. To Stand Prior to attention, it is only necessary to steadily observe and understand and "Radically" transcend the essence of attention, which is the simple, thoughtless heart-feeling of relatedness that is (naturally) associated with the right side of the heart.

When this has become stably clear and Perfectly obvious to you (through real practice of the Way of the Heart in the progressive developmental stages of the Yoga of "Consideration"), such that you have no other or contrary motives (or binding attachments to the psycho-physical point of view characteristic of the first five stages of life), then you may meditate thus: Constantly submit to feel (rather than put attention on) the thoughtless feeling of relatedness. Do this moment to moment, rather than follow attention itself. In every moment of this simple and easeful feeling-inspection, understand the feeling of relatedness to be self-contraction (and thus transcend it, by Feeling Prior to it), or simply Feel into (and, spontaneously, Beyond) the heart-feeling of relatedness, and thus Feel That In Which the feeling of relatedness is arising (or In Which or Of Which the feeling of relatedness is a contraction).

What Is That In Which the thoughtless feeling of relatedness is arising? What Is That In Which or Of Which the thoughtless feeling of relatedness is an apparent contraction? By Grace, Feel, "Locate", and Be That, Until It Gracefully Reveals Its Own Nature, Status, and Inherent Love-Bliss, even to the degree that all apparently arising conditions are Always Already Divinely Recognizable In and As That.

Consciousness Itself Prior to (or Free of) all apparent modifications (gross, subtle, and causal) Is Inherent Love-Bliss (or Self-Existing and Self-Radiant Happiness). If any apparent modification arises, the Self-Existing and Self-Radiant Being (Itself), or Consciousness Itself, or Happiness Itself, is apparently diminished, or limited and reduced to the quality of that gross, subtle, or causal modification. Therefore, Be, Free of all modifications. Stand Free and Be Free of identification with the body, the mind, the total body-mind, and all the worlds of the apparent relations of these illusory or merely apparent versions of conditional, or limited and temporary, selfhood. Stand and Be, Free As the One (or the Transcendental and Inherently Spiritual Divine Self-Condition) Who is apparently Witnessing and Who is apparently modified by or as all that arises conditionally. Even When you (by self-transcending response to Grace) Have Realized (and Are Awake As) That Very and Self-Existing and Self-Radiant Consciousness, simply Abide As That, and allow all apparent conditions to arise and pass as they will, but (rather than cling to or follow what arises) simply and spontaneously (and Divinely) Recognize whatever arises. In this manner, let all apparent conditions be Felt As Is, or Felt Beyond, as if they are, all together, like a shawl of gauze, or an insubstantial vapor, transparent to the Inherent Self-Light. Do This, and all this conditional seeming will be Divinely Transfigured, Divinely Transformed, and, finally, Outshined in "Bright" (Divine) Love-Bliss, or the Self-Existing and Self-Radiant and Unqualified Feeling of Being That Is Absolute Consciousness Itself.

XVI

The separate "I" is conditional, dependent, and necessarily in relationship.

The separate "I" only perceives (or experiences) and conceives (or knows).

Perception and conception (or all experiencing and knowing, whether active or passive) arise via (and as) a systematic (and unnecessary) self-limitation (or a generalized self-contraction) of the conditional, or separate, "I".

When self-contraction (or all self-limitation of and as the conditional "I") is understood as such, and all perception and conception (or all relations, all others, all objects, all sensations, and all thoughts) are thence felt beyond, only the feeling of relatedness itself remains as the obvious (prior to all perception and conception).

The conditional "I" is not a separate Absolute.

The conditional "I" is not the Inherent (or Native) Feeling of Being.

The conditional "I" is not Consciousness Itself.

The conditional "I" is not Happiness (Itself).

The conditional, or separate, "I" is the simple (or mere) feeling of relatedness.

The feeling of relatedness is (itself) the separate "I" itself.

The feeling of relatedness is the essence (or the essential and prior feeling) that is otherwise (via intensified self-contraction) perceived and conceived as the body-mind (or the apparent psycho-physical "I"), or all apparent conditions, things, and others, or all apparent relations of the feeling of relatedness (which is the essence of the separate "I", immediate and prior to the apparent body-mind and all apparent relations of the body-mind).

The feeling of relatedness is the event of the arising of the separate "I".

The feeling of relatedness, which is the ego-"I", is the essential (or original) self-contraction.

Therefore, if the root-contraction that is the feeling of relatedness is understood as such (as self-contraction), and if the feeling of relatedness is (thence) Relinquished in its Perfectly Subjective Source, then the ego-"I" itself is (Inherently, and Inherently Perfectly) transcended.

If the ego-"I" (or self-contraction itself), which is the feeling of relatedness itself, is Relinquished in its Perfectly Subjective Source, only the Inherent (or Native) Feeling of Being remains as the Obvious (Prior to perception, body, conception, mind, self-contraction, emotional recoil, self-limitation, the feeling of relatedness, the feeling of "difference", the ego-"I", or separate self, the object, the other, the world, even all relations, and conditional existence itself).

The Inherent (or Native) Feeling of Being Merely <u>Is</u>.

The Inherent (or Native) Feeling of Being <u>Is</u> That Which Inherently Transcends the ego-"I", conditionality, dependence, and relatedness.

The Inherent (or Native) Feeling of Being <u>Is</u> Existence Itself.

The Inherent (or Native) Feeling of Being <u>Is</u> Consciousness Itself.

The Inherent (or Native) Feeling of Being <u>Is</u> Mere Radiance, Self-Radiant and Inherently Existing.

The Inherent (or Native) Feeling of Being <u>Is</u> Self-Existing and Infinite (or Unqualified) Love-Bliss, Which <u>Is</u> Happiness Itself.

The Inherent (or Native) Feeling of Being <u>Is</u> the Eternal and Un-Threatened and Perfectly Subjective Reality, Without a defined center (or an egoic and conditional self), and Without any limits, shapes, or boundaries.

The Inherent (or Native) Feeling of Being, or Unqualified Love-Bliss Itself, <u>Is</u> God, Truth, and Reality (or Who <u>Is</u> and What <u>Is</u>, As or "Where" It <u>Is</u>).

The Inherent (or Native) Feeling of Being, or Unqualified Love-Bliss, <u>Is</u> the Heart Itself, the Divine Self-Domain, or the "Bright".

The Inherent (or Native) Feeling of Being, or Unqualified Love-Bliss, <u>Is</u> the Way of the Heart Itself.

XVII

The feeling of relatedness is not itself (or merely) an idea (or a concept in mind).

The feeling of relatedness is an activity.

The feeling of relatedness is the primal or first activity, and, therefore, it is the cause and the pivotal referent of all subsequent activities (including the activities of mind).

The feeling of relatedness is the activity of self-contraction, which effectively causes all subsequent activities (including the effort not to act).

The feeling of relatedness (or the self-contraction) becomes (or is reflected as) the presumption (or idea) of the separate "other" and the presumption (or idea) of the separate "I".

The presumption (or idea) of the separate "I" (or the ego-"I") does not arise independently, but it always, necessarily, and inherently arises coincident with the presumption (or idea) of the separate "other" (related to the separate "I").

Therefore, egoity (or the ego-"I") is not merely or originally an independent entity, category, idea, perception, or experience, but it is the primary consequence of the uninspected feeling of relatedness.

The ego-"I" does not exist outside the context of relatedness.

The ego-"I" is relatedness (or the sign of relationship, rather than of an original entity existing prior to relatedness and relationship), but the ego-"I" (which is self-contraction, and, therefore, self-contracted, or avoiding relationship) is inherently ambivalent toward relatedness itself and every specific kind or context of relationship.

The ego-"I" is "Narcissus", or the self-bondage that results from self-contraction (or the flight from the "other").

The ego-"I" is not a beginning but a necessarily un-Happy result.

The ego-"I" is, simply, a reaction to the implied "other" (or the presumed and otherwise experienced object or context of relatedness) in any moment, and there is no ego-"I" (or separate self idea) without (or except as) a reaction to the implied "other".

The separate "I" and its "other" are not inherent categories of existence.

Rather, the separate "I" and its "other" (in any moment) are added to (or superimposed upon) existence as (or by) a reaction to the conditional perception of existence.

Once this reaction (or self-contraction) is generated, suffering (or every form of contracted existence, or contraction from the Native or Always Already Given Condition of Transcendental and Inherently Spiritual and Necessarily Divine Self-Existence, or Perfectly Subjective Being Itself) inevitably follows.

Therefore, egoity (or the suffered drama of the separate "I" and its separate "other") is a disease (even an imaginary disease, since it is self-caused, unnecessary, and self-contained).

The fascinating "I" (separate, independent of any "other" and the process of relationship) is the ultimate psychological and philosophical Illusion.

There Is no separate "I".

Therefore, there Is no separate "other" (or any condition that is separate from "I", since the separate "I" is itself an Illusion).

The separate "I" and the separate "other" are presumptions (or ideas) generated by a feeling-contraction (or an unnecessary and generally uninspected reaction to the conditional perception of existence in any moment).

Therefore, the imaginary disease that is egoity can be transcended in any present moment, if self-contraction (in its progression, or "Circle", of forms, and, ultimately, in the form of the feeling of relatedness itself) is presently observed (and Relinquished in its Perfectly Subjective Source).

If the separate "I" and its separate "other" are Relinquished (or Perfectly transcended) in any present moment, so that the complex presumption of separate "I" and separate "other", or the feeling of relatedness itself, is transcended (and is not superimposed on what otherwise arises, or on what is otherwise perceived conditionally), then what arises?

If conditions arise, but no separate "I"-"other" feeling is added to what arises, then what arises?

It is not that, in that case, there are no perceptions of conditions, but all conditions (including the perceiving body-mind) are Comprehended (or Perfectly Felt) prior to the self-contraction and its "I"-"other" structure of feeling, perceiving, and presuming.

Therefore, if the separate (and separative) "I"-"other" presumption is not added to what arises, what arises appears only As it Is, or Inherently Free of the feeling-concept of inherent separateness (or "difference").

This Unique and Original Freedom may be likened to the perception of waves from the point of view of the ocean (as compared to the perception of waves from the point of view of any single wave).

If any conditional pattern In What Is becomes a point of view (or the point of view) Toward What Is, then What Is ceases to Be Obvious, and the pattern merely perceives itself (separately, or "differently", over against all other patterns).

If the separate "I" becomes the point of view, then the "other" is everywhere multiplied and perceived, and only the stress of the separate "I"-"other" confrontation is experienced and known.

However, if the separate conditional point of view is transcended, and What Is (Prior to it) becomes the Disposition In Which all conditions (including the perceiving body-mind) are observed, then the pattern of conditions is no longer a problem, a dilemma, or a confrontation of "one" (or the separate "I") against an "other", but the pattern of conditions is an inherently problem-free totality (or an open sea of motions).

In the totality thus perceived, there is no separation, even if manifold complexity is (apparently) perceived.

There are no separate waters in the sea, but every wave or motion folds in one another on the Deep.

Such is the Disposition of the seventh stage of life.

124

In the seventh stage of life, whatever arises conditionally (including the conditional body-mind) is Divinely Recognized As it Is (or In and Of and As Self-Existing and Self-Radiant Consciousness Itself, Which Is the Deep Ocean of all apparent events).

In the seventh stage of life, whatever otherwise (or from the conventional, or psycho-physical, point of view) appears to arise separately (as body-mind, or "I", or "other", or "thing", or even the feeling of relatedness itself, or the feeling of "difference" itself) is Divinely Recognized In and As Consciousness Itself (or That Which Always Already Exists As One and the totality).

Therefore, in the seventh stage of life, the feeling of relatedness, or the feeling of "difference", or the ideas of separate "I" and separate "other", or the activity of self-contraction itself, or all suffering (or problem, or dilemma), is not the point of view (nor the result of a separate point of view), but the (apparent) feeling of relatedness, the (apparent) feeling of "difference", the (apparent) ideas of "I" and "other", the (apparent) self-contraction, and all (apparent) suffering register only on the Deep of Self-Existing and Self-Radiant Consciousness Itself.

In the seventh stage of life, the feeling of relatedness (or, Ultimately, or Most Simply, the most tacit feeling of "difference") Is Divinely Recognized, Inherently Transcended, and, Ultimately, Outshined In the Perfectly Subjective Feeling of Being (or Love-Bliss Itself).

In the seventh stage of life, all conditions (or all motions, or patterns, or waves of Spirit-Energy) Are (each in their moment) Divinely Recognized On and In and As the Deep (or Self-Existing and Self-Radiant Consciousness Itself, or Perfectly Subjective Being Itself), and That Divine Recognition Is Itself a Force (or "Bright" Vision) That Progressively Outshines the Play of motions (or the apparent modifications of the Self-Existing and Self-Radiant Shine of Love-Bliss).

Therefore, Deep Recognition Realizes Only Self-Existing and Self-Radiant Love-Bliss where the conditional patterns of merely apparent modification rise and fall in their folds.

At first this Realization Shines in the world and Plays "Bright" Demonstrations on the waves.

Ultimately, the "Brightness" Is Indifferent (Beyond "difference") In the Deep, There Where Primitive relatedness Is Freely Drowned, and When "Bright" Recognition Rests Most Deeply In Its Fathomless Shine, the Play of motions Is Translated In Love-Bliss, Pervasive In the Water-Stand, and, like a Sea of Blankets, All the Deep Unfolds To Waken In the Once Neglected (Now Un-Covered) Light of Self-Illuminated and Eternal Day.

XVIII

Only Self-Existing and Self-Radiant Consciousness Itself Is. All that appears to be not-Consciousness (or an object of Consciousness) is an apparition produced by apparent modification (or spontaneous contraction and perturbation) of the Inherent Radiance (or Native Love-Bliss) of Consciousness Itself.

If any object (or apparent modification) is Divinely Recognized By, In, and As Consciousness Itself, there is no binding capability in the object, and it is (Directly) Transcended and (Ultimately) Outshined In the "Bright" Love-Bliss That Is Consciousness Itself.

Even so, once objects (or conditions) arise, they tend to persist (or to demand repetition), and Consciousness may, therefore, tend to dwell on them with fascination.

When objective persistence is encountered, Consciousness may tend to appear to be implicated. Thus, desire arises, both for and against the various kinds of past, present, or possible modifications. And desire tends to weaken (or to replace) the Transcendental Self-Power of Divine Recognition.

When Divine Recognition fails, Consciousness ceases to Abide In Its Own (or Inherent) Love-Bliss, or Happiness Itself, and It dwells instead in the various qualities of apparent objects, both positive and negative.

Arising objects are never exclusively positive or exclusively negative in their quality.

Objects arise by apparent contraction of the One Self-Existing and Self-Radiant Field of Being (Itself), and contraction of the Single Field (or any single field) always results in dynamic perturbation, or an apparition of opposing forces.

If objects arise, they arise in a dynamic order, Grounded in the One Love-Bliss, but apparent only in a play of oppositions (or dynamic flows). Therefore, if objects arise, both positive and negative arise. And if objects are not Divinely Recognized, they persist (and become more and more complex) through dynamic desires (both for and against, depending on whether the quality of an object is regarded to be positive or negative).

All of this arising is an Illusion, the principal signs of which are the presumption of relatedness (and of "difference"), the presumption of a separate self, the positive desire for some things or relations, the negative desire to avoid some other things and relations, the non-Recognition of all things and relations, the general absence or diminishment of Love-Bliss (or Inherent Happiness), the obsessive search for Love-Bliss (or constant Free Happiness), the inability to strategically escape the double bind (or apparently inherent problem) of conditional existence and conditional motivations (or the inability to strategically escape or transcend the apparently objective worlds), and, thus, the inability to avoid the inevitable result of all of this, which is self-despair and self-death.

This Illusion can be understood and transcended.

The understanding of this Illusion (as Illusion) is simply a matter of observing It (rather than desiring or avoiding what arises).

The transcendence of this Illusion is simply a matter of Divinely Recognizing whatever arises (until arising is itself Outshined).

The conditional self tends to seek (or to pursue and to avoid) rather than to observe. Therefore, I Appear, in order to

Reveal the Way whereby intelligent attention may observe all conditional arising, so the Heart may understand self-contraction (and transcend even attention itself).

The conditional self tends to persist as self-contraction (motivated by non-Recognition, presumed problems, positive and negative desires, and every kind of seeking). Therefore, I Appear, in order to Bless (or to Be Merely Present), so that the Spiritual Power of Love-Bliss That Inherently Transcends the conditional self may Attract and Awaken the Heart to the Inherent Feeling of Being (Itself).

I Reveal the Way of the Heart to all (by My Work and My Word and My Sign[29]), and I Bless all (by Heart), so that the Illusion of conditional existence may be transcended by all (through Awakening to Consciousness Itself and Its Inherent Power of Divine Recognition, or Its Inherent and Always Already Perfect Transcendence of the Illusion of self-contraction and the Illusion of conditional worlds).

Understanding and transcendence of separate self, and of all seeking (or all pursuing and avoiding), and of all relations (or worlds) cannot be achieved <u>by</u> the separate self, nor by seeking (whether by pursuit or by avoidance), nor by experience or knowledge of any relations or worlds.

Understanding and transcendence are necessarily associated with Graceful Help, Profound Instruction, and Free Blessing, and these Awaken (Ultimately, Perfect) self-observation (which, rather than seeking, and rather than animating self-contraction, merely <u>observes</u> all seeking and all self-contraction). Therefore, if My Word and My Person are served by attentive listening, and if My Revealing Voice and Sign (or My Revealing bodily human Form, and My Spiritual, and Always Blessing, Presence, and My Very, and Inherently Perfect, State) are (by attentive lis-

29. Heart-Master Da Love-Ananda Proclaims that His own bodily (human) Form Is Itself the Teaching. By this He means that His own Divinely Transfigured, Divinely Transformed, and Divinely Indifferent body-mind Perfectly Incarnates and Reveals the Divine Person, Who is the Truth of all beings. In the heart-acknowledgement of the Sign that is Heart-Master Da's bodily appearing (human) Form (which paradoxically includes or represents His Spiritual, and Always Blessing, Presence and His State of Transcendental Consciousness), we are Awakened to the intuition of our own Divine Self-Nature.

tening) truly heard, and if My Heart-Revealing Sign (or Person) is then (clearly) seen (As the Divine Person), and if listening and hearing and seeing are really practiced, the <u>search</u> for understanding and transcendence has become unnecessary (by Grace).

This Grace (Given by Me, and Received by My devotee, even from the beginning of the Way of the Heart) directly Awakens self-understanding, and this Grace more and more becomes (or is Found to Be) an Attraction beyond self-contraction, until Consciousness Itself is Realized (and Its Inherent "Bright" Power of Divine Recognition, Inherently Free of all "difference", then Outshines all worlds).

May all those who Listen To Me Be Blessed To Hear Me. May all those who Hear Me and See Me Practice To The Perfect Degree Of Divine Self-Realization In The Free Radiance Of My "Bright" Heart.

May all those who Suffer The Bondage Of attention Be Released By The Power Of My Mere and Blessing Presence.

Let The Heart-Power Released Through This Blessing Act Be Sufficient For The Liberation Of all beings.

Let It Be So.

A Guide to the Sacred Esoteric Language of the Way of the Heart

advanced and ultimate

Sri Da Avabhasa uses the term "advanced" to describe the practice of devotees in the Way of the Heart (or of practitioners in any other tradition) who practice in the fourth stage of life and the fifth stage of life. These are individuals who have Awakened to the Divine as the tangible, All-Pervading Presence, or Radiant Spirit-Force or Person, with Which they live in a constant relationship of devotion, or Love-Communion. Practitioners in the advanced stages of the Way of the Heart have been Awakened to responsibility for feeling-Contemplation of Sri Da Avabhasa's Spiritual (and Always Blessing) Presence as well as His bodily (human) Form.

Sri Da Avabhasa reserves the word "ultimate" to describe the practice of His devotees (and of practitioners in any other tradition) in the sixth stage of life and the seventh stage of life, or individuals who practice in the Domain of Consciousness Itself. Practitioners in the ultimate stages of the Way of the Heart have been Awakened to responsibility for feeling-Contemplation of Sri Da Avabhasa's Very (and Inherently Perfect) State, as well as His Spiritual (and Always Blessing) Presence and His bodily (human) Form.

"advanced" context of the fourth stage of life (See **"original", "basic", and "advanced" contexts of the fourth stage of life**.)

Aham Sphurana

"Aham" is a Sanskrit term that means "I", and it refers to the Transcendental Self-Identity. "Sphurana" means "spring forth" or "shine".

Aham Sphurana is a traditional designation for the manifesting Current of Love-Bliss that (Sri Da Avabhasa has Revealed) is first associated with the body-mind at a point in the right side of the heart, but which is truly Transcendental, Unbounded, and All-Pervading.

Ajna Door

The Ajna Door, also known as the "single eye", the "mystic eye", or the "third eye", is the subtle psychic center or chakra located between and behind the eyebrows and associated with the brain core. The awakening of the ajna chakra may give rise to mystical visions and intuitive reflections of other realms of experience within and outside the individual. The ajna chakra governs the higher mind, will, vision, and conception. It is sometimes also referred to as the "Guru's Seat", the psychic center through which the Heart-Master contacts his (or her) devotee with his Spirit-Baptism or Blessing.

Akasha

The Sanskrit word "akasha" means "clear-space", or "sky", and also the etheric, or subtlest, element of existence. In Heart-Master Da Love-Ananda's use here, it refers to the conditional, and therefore temporary, intuition of the Spiritual Light of Transcendental Consciousness in fifth stage

131

conditional Nirvikalpa Samadhi, or a moment of unqualified enjoyment of the free Radiance, or "Shine", that is the Divine Source-Condition.

Alpha and Omega

Sri Da Avabhasa uses the term "Omega" to characterize the materialistic anti-Spiritual culture that today dominates both West and East. The Omega, or Occidental, or Western, strategy is motivated to the attainment of a future-time, perfected ordering and fulfillment of the conditionally appearing worlds through the intense application of human invention, political will, and even Divine Influence. It is analogous to the left hemisphere and the analytical functions of the brain.

Sri Da Avabhasa calls the characteristically Oriental, or Eastern, strategy the "Alpha strategy". Just as Omega cultures seek to perfect and fulfill the world, Alpha cultures pursue an original or non-temporal and undisturbed peace, in which the world is absent (and thus unimposing). The Alpha strategy is analogous to the right hemisphere and the synthetic or holistic functions of the brain. Although the cultures that were originally founded on the Alpha approach to life and Truth are fast disappearing, the Alpha strategy remains the archetype of Spiritual life, even in the Omega culture.

Neither the Omega strategy nor the Alpha strategy Realizes Truth, as each is rooted in the yet to be inspected, observed, and understood action of egoity itself, which motivates all human interests short of Divine Self-Realization. Both the Omega and the Alpha strategies only dramatize the ego's desire for escape and fulfillment, and thus each tends to perpetuate the ego itself.

Arrow

In profound, deep meditation, the Spirit-Current may be felt in the form of the Arrow, or as Sri Da Avabhasa explains, "a motionless axis that seems to stand in the center of the body, between the frontal and spinal lines".

"Atma-Murti"

In Sanskrit, "atma" means both the individual (essential, or conditional) self and the Divine Self. In Sri Da Avabhasa's term "Atma-Murti", "Atma" indicates the Transcendental, Inherently Spiritual, and

Divine Self, and "Murti" means "Form", or "Formed of", or "the Form of". Thus, "Atma-Murti" literally means "the Form (Murti) That Is the (Very) Divine Self (Atman)". And, as Sri Da Avabhasa Indicates everywhere in His Wisdom-Teaching, "Atma-Murti" refers to the Sat-Guru (and the Very Self of all), "Located" as "the Feeling of Being (Itself)."

"basic" context of the fourth stage of life (See "original", "basic", and "advanced" contexts of the fourth stage of life.)

Bhakti Yoga

The Yoga of devotion (bhakti) or reunion with the Divine via expressed devotional love, most typically directed to a Spiritual Adept (living or deceased), or to a mythological or symbolic personage representing the Divine Self-Condition.

bindu

In the esoteric Yogic traditions of India, bindu (literally "drop" or "point" in Sanskrit) is a point without spatial or temporal dimension in which all manifest forms, energies, and universes are ultimately coalesced or expressed. Bindu, or "zero"-point, is said to exist at each level or plane of psycho-physical reality.

bodily base

The bodily base is principally associated with the muladhara chakra, the lowest energy plexus (chakra) in the human bodymind, at the base of the spine (or the general region including and immediately above the perineum). In many Yogic traditions, the bodily base is regarded to be the seat of the latent ascending Spiritual Current, or Kundalini. Sat-Guru Da Avabhasa Reveals that, in fact, the Spirit-Current must first be breathed down to the bodily base through the frontal line before it can effectively be directed into the ascending, spinal course.

the "Bright", "Brightness"

Since His Illumined boyhood, Sat-Guru Da Love-Ananda has used the term the "Bright" (and its variations, such as "Brightness") to describe the Blissfully Self-Luminous Divine Being, eternally, infinitely, and inherently Self-Radiant, Which He knew even then as the All-Pervading, Transcendental, Inherently Spiritual, and Divine Reality of His own body-mind and of all beings, things, and worlds.

causal (See **gross, subtle, causal.**)

causal stress

Heart-Master Da Avabhasa's descriptive term for the causal knot, the root-contraction of identification with the egoic self, felt as suffering and un-Happiness, but ultimately Realized to be the feeling of relatedness itself, or the root activity of attention.

celibate renunciation, formal

Formal celibate renunciation is practiced by devotees in the first actually seeing stage of the Way of the Heart and beyond who choose and are suited to this form of renunciate discipline. Through the Grace of Sri Da Avabhasa and His Blessing of their choice, these devotees voluntarily and motivelessly relinquish all sexual activity, and its associated relational obligations, in body, mind, and speech.

Circle

The Circle is a primary circuit or passageway of the Living Spirit-Current and the natural bodily energy as they flow through the body-mind. The Circle is composed of two arcs: the descending Current associated with the frontal line, or the more physically oriented dimension, of the body-mind; and the ascending Current associated with the spinal line, or the more mentally and subtly oriented dimension, of the body-mind. When both these portions of the Circle are free of obstruction, the body-mind is harmoniously surrendered into the Current of Spirit-Life and full of Its Radiant Love-Bliss.

"conductivity"

Sri Da Avabhasa's technical term for those disciplines in the Way of the Heart through which the body-mind is aligned and submitted to the natural life-energy of the cosmos (in its association with the individual body-mind), and, for those who are Spiritually Awakened, to the Spirit-Current of Divine Life.

Practitioners of the Way of the Heart practice participation in and responsibility for the movement of natural bodily energies associated with the body-mind and, when they become Spiritually Awakened

practitioners, the movement of the Spirit-Current in its natural course of association with the body-mind, via intentional exercises of feeling and breathing.

"conscious exercise"

"Conscious exercise", as described in *Conscious Exercise and the Transcendental Sun,* by Heart-Master Da Love-Ananda, is the basic practical discipline underlying all other practical disciplines in the Way of the Heart. Founded in awakening feeling-Contemplation of Heart-Master Da's bodily (human) Form, His Spiritual (and Always Blessing) Presence, and His Very (and Inherently Perfect) State, throughout daily life and in two daily periods of formal physical exercise, the practitioner of "conscious exercise" integrates body, life-force, and mind, or attention, through persistent feeling-surrender into the all-pervading field of life-energy. "Conscious exercise" includes disciplines of posture and breathing and is a practical science of love in ordinary life.

"conscious process"

Sri Da Avabhasa's technical term for those practices in the Way of the Heart through which the mind or attention is controlled and turned about (from conventional self-involvement) to feeling-Contemplation of the bodily (human) Form, the Spiritual (and Always Blessing) Presence, and the Very (and Inherently Perfect) State of Sri Da Avabhasa (and, thus and thereby, of the Divine Person). It is the senior discipline and responsibility of all practitioners in the Way of the Heart.

"consideration"

Sri Da Avabhasa's technical term for the "process of one-pointed but ultimately thoughtless concentration and exhaustive contemplation of a particular object, function, person, process, or condition, until the essence or ultimate obviousness of that subject is clear". As engaged in the Way of the Heart, "consideration" is not merely an intellectual investigation. It is the participatory investment of one's whole being. If one "considers" something fully in the context of one's practice of feeling-Contemplation of Sat-Guru Da, this concentration results "in both the highest intuition and the most practical grasp of the Lawful and Divine necessities of human existence".

Cosmic Mandala

"Mandala" (literally, "circle") is commonly used in the esoteric Spiritual traditions to describe the levels of cosmic existence. It also denotes an artistic rendering of interior visions of the cosmos. Sri Da Avabhasa uses the phrase "Cosmic Mandala" to describe the totality of the conditional cosmos, which appears in vision as concentric circles of light, progressing from red at the perimeter through golden-yellow, silvery white, indigo or black, and brilliant blue, to the Ultimate White Brilliance in the Mandala's center.

Da

In *The Dawn Horse Testament*, chapter 27, Sri Da Avabhasa Says:

"Da" Is A Traditional Name Of God, or A Traditional Feeling-Reference To The Ultimate Condition and Power Of Existence. "Da" Is An Eternal, Ancient, and Always New Name For The Divine Being, Source, and Spirit-Power, and "Da" Is An Eternal, Ancient, and Always New Name For The Realizer Who Reveals (and Is The Revelation Of) The Divine Being, Source, and Spirit-Power. Therefore, The Name "Da" Is (Since The Ancient Days) Found In Religious Cultures All Over the world.

As An Expression Of My Realization Of The Eternal, Ancient, and Always New One, I Am Given The Name "Da" (As A Sign Of The One Of Whom I Am The Realizer, The Revealer, and The Revelation).

Devotional Way of Faith

The Devotional Way of Insight and the Devotional Way of Faith are the two forms of practice that characterize meditative feeling-Contemplation of Heart-Master Da Avabhasa in the Way of the Heart.

The Devotional Way of Faith is a technical process of (primarily) feeling and faith, whereby the practitioner is heart-Attracted by Sri Da Avabhasa's bodily (human) Form, His Spiritual (and Always Blessing) Presence, and His Very (and Inherently Perfect) State to feel beyond the self-contraction and is thereby spontaneously awakened to self-understanding and self-transcendence.

Devotional Way of Insight

Through a technical process of (primarily) feeling and insight, the practitioner of the Devotional Way of Insight, while feeling-Contemplating the bodily (human) Form, the Spiritual (and Always Blessing) Presence, and the Very (and Inherently Perfect) State of Sri Da Avabhasa, observes, understands, and then feels beyond the self-contraction into Divine Communion.

Divine Recognition

Sat-Guru Da Avabhasa's technical term for the Inherent and Most Perfect comprehension and perception, Awakened in the seventh stage of life, that all phenomena (including body, mind, and conventional self) are merely (apparent) modifications of the Self-Existing and Self-Radiant Divine Person.

Divine Self-Domain

Sri Da Avabhasa Affirms that there is a Divine Domain that is the "Bright" Destiny of every Realizer of the Divine Self. It is not elsewhere, not a place like a subtle heaven or mythical paradise, but It is the always present, Transcendental, Inherently Spiritual, Divine Self of every conditional self, and the Radiant Source-Condition of every conditional place.

Because the God-World, or Realm of Self-Light, transcends even the most heavenly dimensions of conditional space-time, it is beyond the manifest mind's capacity to experience, describe, or comprehend. Sat-Guru Da Love-Ananda Reveals that the Divine Self-Domain is not other than the Heart.

Divine Star

Sri Da Avabhasa and the "Bright" Heart-Radiance of God may appear to an individual as a brilliant white five-pointed Star, the primal conditional Representation, or Sign, of the "Bright", the Source-Energy, or Divine Light, of which all conditional phenomena and the total cosmos are modifications.

The apparently objective Divine Star necessarily exists and can potentially be experienced in every moment and location in cosmic Nature. However, the vision of the Divine Star is not a necessary experience for growth in the Spiritual process or for Divine Realization.

Divine Transfiguration, Divine Transformation, Divine Indifference, Divine Translation

In Sri Da Avabhasa's Way of the Heart, these are the four phases of the Enlightened Yoga of the seventh, or Divinely Self-Realized, stage of life.

When Divine Enlightenment is firmly established, the body-mind of the Realizer is first progressively relaxed into, or pervaded by, the inherent Radiance of the Spiritual and Transcendental Divine Self. This process of Divine Transfiguration expresses itself as the Realizer's active Spiritual Blessing in all relationships.

When the gross body-mind is Full in this Transfiguring process, Divine Transformation begins, wherein the deeper (or psychic, subtler mental, and root-egoic) dimensions of the body-mind are Infused with that same unqualified "Brightness" of Divine Being. This Transformation spontaneously yields extraordinary psycho-physical signs, such as the capability to heal, physical longevity, mental genius, and the profound manifestation of true Wisdom and selfless Love.

Such Divinization is not to be confused with the evolutionary Spiritual processes awakened via advanced Yogic meditation, which may yield apparently similar psycho-physical results or expressions, but which are still founded on the ego's exploitation of the Divine Spirit-Energy. (See chapter 7 of *The Enlightenment of the Whole Body* for further discussion by Sri Da Avabhasa of this important distinction.)

In the phase of Divine Indifference all attention and the whole body-mind are brought to most profound rest in the "Brightness" of the Divine Self, and the Realizer Freely Radiates universal Heart-Blessing, but spontaneously Free of even Enlightened concern for (or interest in) conditional objects, relations, and states.

In the Way of the Heart, and as Demonstrated by Sri Da Avabhasa, such Divine Indifference stands in contrast to the asceticism that motivates much of the traditional practice of strategic dissociation from the states and relations of the body-mind. Divine Indifference is the transition to the culminating phase of Divine Self-Realization, which is Divine Translation, or, as Heart-Master Da Love-Ananda also calls it, Outshining.

The four phases of the Yoga of Divine Enlightenment are discussed fully by Heart-Master Da Love-Ananda in chapters 43 and 44 of *The Dawn Horse Testament*.

"Easy Prayer"

The "Easy Prayer" of Spiritual Invocation of Da Avabhasa, Spiritual Feeling-Contemplation of Him, and Surrender to His Spiritual Grace is "Radiant Da, Giver Of Life, I Surrender". It is Given to practitioners of the Devotional Way of Faith in practicing stage two of the technically "fully elaborated" form of the Way of the Heart, who are responding to Sri Da Avabhasa's Spiritual (and Always Blessing) Presence. Sri Da Avabhasa summarizes His Instructions on the "Easy Prayer" in *The Dawn Horse Testament*.

etheric body

The universal energy, magnetism, and space that surrounds and pervades every physical body; in practical terms our sense of vitality and our emotional-sexual, feeling nature. It functions through and corresponds to the nervous system. The etheric body mediates between the conscious mind and the physical being, distributing energy, and controlling the body-mind's use of energy and emotion. It is the dimension of vitality, or life-force. We feel it not only as vital energy and power and magnetic-gravitational forces, but also as the endless play of emotional polarization, positive and negative, to everything that arises.

Feeling of Being

The Feeling of Being is the uncaused (or Self-Existing), Self-Radiant, and unqualified feeling-intuition of the Transcendental, Inherently Spiritual, and, ultimately, Divine Self. This absolute Feeling does not merely accompany or express the Realization of the Heart Itself, but it is identical to that Realization. To feel, or, really, to Be, the Feeling of Being is to enjoy the Love-Bliss of Absolute Consciousness, Which, when Most Perfectly Realized, cannot be prevented or even diminished either by the events of life or by death.

feeling of relatedness

Sri Da Avabhasa's technical term for the root-feeling of separation, separateness, and separativeness, the feeling of "difference", the essence of self-contraction, or the avoidance of relationship. It is the essence of attention itself, the root structure or activity that is ego. It is Most Perfectly transcended in Divine Self-Realization.

The feeling of relatedness is a primary subject of the final sections of *The ego-"I" is the Illusion of Relatedness.*

Feeling-Enquiry (See **Hridaya-Vichara, Feeling-Enquiry.**)

first actually seeing stage

In the first actually seeing stage of the Way of the Heart, the Spiritual conversion of body, emotion, and mind to a life of Divine Communion (which was established in the would-be-seeing stage) is now the basic disposition of the practitioner. This Spiritual capability matures by Grace through the practitioner's ever-increasing devotional surrender to Sri Da Avabhasa's Spiritual (and Always Blessing) Presence. Through this devotional surrender, the Spirit-Current is allowed to more and more deeply infuse the frontal line and, thereby, to purify and Spiritualize the gross body and the gross personality.

"fully elaborated" (or "elaborately detailed") form of the Way of the Heart, the technically

Heart-Master Da Avabhasa Offers two forms of the progressive process of Perfectly self-transcending God-Realization in the Way of the Heart to account for the differences in individuals' inclinations and capabilities for the technical details of Spiritual practice.

Sri Da Avabhasa refers to the most detailed practice of the Way of the Heart as the "technically 'fully elaborated'" form of practice, which develops and, over time, demonstrates, all the Yogic and other classic signs of Spiritual, Transcendental, and Divine Awakening. Each successive stage of practice in the technically "fully elaborated" form of the Way of the Heart is likewise defined by progressively more detailed responsibilities, disciplines, and practice that must be assumed in order to take responsibility for the signs of growing maturity in the process of Divine Awakening.

Uniquely exemplary practitioners, for whom this more intensive approach and more technically detailed discipline of attention and energy are effective as self-transcending practice, enter The (Free Daist) Lay Renunciate Order, and they are Called to demonstrate exemplary self-renunciation via an increasingly economized discipline of body, mind, and speech, and to maximize their growth in meditative self-surrender, self-forgetting, and self-transcendence through feeling-Contemplation of Da Avabhasa. The progress of practice in the technically "fully elaborated" form of the Way of the Heart is monitored, measured, and evaluated by stages through the devotee's participatory submission to the sacred culture of either The Lay Renunciate Order or, for the most exemplary practitioners in the ultimate stages of life, The Naitauba (Free Daist) Order of Sannyasins (also called "The Free Renunciate Order").

"great path of return"

Sri Da Avabhasa characterizes the traditional religious and Spiritual paths of the first six stages of life as the "great path of return", because the traditional methods of the un-Enlightened stages of life seek to regress, or return, to a specific, or absolute, Goal, which is often termed "God", "Truth", "Reality", etc. In the uniquely self-transcending, or "Radical", practice of the Way of the Heart, all Goals and all motivated methods of either progress or regress are to be persistently observed, understood, and transcended.

Great Tradition

Sat-Guru Da Love-Ananda's term for the total inheritance of human cultural, religious, magical, mystical, Spiritual, Transcendental, and Divine paths, philosophies, and testimonies from all the eras and cultures of humanity, which has (in the present era of worldwide communication) become the common legacy of humankind.

gross, subtle, causal

Heart-Master Da Avabhasa is in agreement with the traditional description that the human body-mind and its environment consist of three great dimensions—gross, subtle, and causal.

The gross, or most physical, dimension is associated with what Sat-Guru Da calls the "frontal line" of the human body-mind, or the descended processes of psycho-physical embodiment and experience in the waking state.

The subtle dimension, which is senior to and pervades the gross dimension, includes the etheric (or energic), lower mental (or verbal-intentional and lower psychic), and higher mental (or deeper psychic, mystical, and discriminative) aspects of the being. The subtle dimension is associated primarily with the spinal line (and only secondarily with the frontal line) of the body-mind, including the brain core and the subtle centers of mind in the higher brain. It is also, therefore, associated with the visionary, mystical, and Yogic Spiritual processes encountered in dreams, in ascended or internalized meditative experiences, and during and after the death process.

The causal dimension is senior to and pervades both the gross and subtle dimensions. It is the root of attention, or the feeling of relatedness, or the essence of the separate and separative ego-"I". The causal dimension is associated with the right side of the heart, specifically with the sinoatrial node or pacemaker (the psychophysical source of the heartbeat). Its corresponding state of consciousness is the formless awareness of deep sleep.

Gurudev

A traditional Sanskrit term used as a designation for one's principal Guru. Thus, "Gurudev" is used by devotees of Sri Da Avabhasa, with other devotional Names, Titles, and Designations, as an appropriate and honorable form of address of Him.

Hatha Yoga

A traditional practice engaged with the purpose of achieving harmony, ecstasy, and even Liberation through manipulation of body, breath, and energy, with an accompanying discipline of attention.

Practitioners of the Way of the Heart engage the bodily poses (asanas) and the exercises of control of breath traditional to Hatha Yoga in order to purify, balance, and regenerate the functions of the body-mind, and (in due course) to surrender them to the Spiritual Divine.

hearing

Sri Da Avabhasa's technical term for the intuitive and most fundamental understanding of the self-contraction. Through such most fundamental self-understanding, the practitioner awakens to the unique capability for direct transcendence of the self-contraction and simultaneous intuition of the Divine Person and Self-Condition. Hearing is awakened in the midst of a life of devotion, service, self-discipline, meditation, disciplined study of, or listening to, Sri Da Avabhasa's Teaching Argument, and constant self-surrendering, self-forgetting, and self-transcending feeling-Contemplation of Him.

Hearing is the necessary prerequisite for the Spiritual Realization that Heart-Master Da calls "seeing".

Heart-Master (See **True Heart-Master.**)

the Heart

The Heart is God, the Divine Self, the Divine Reality. Divine Self-Realization is associated with the opening of the primal psycho-physical seat of Consciousness and attention in the right side of the heart, hence the term "the Heart" for the Divine Self.

Sri Da Avabhasa distinguishes the Heart as the ultimate Reality from all the psycho-physiological functions of the organic, bodily heart, as well as from the subtle heart, traditionally known as the "anahata (or heart) chakra". The Heart is not "in" the right side of the human heart, nor is it in or limited to the human heart as a whole, or to the body-mind, or to the world. Rather, the human heart and body-mind and the world exist in the Heart, the Divine Being.

heart chakra

The subtle psychic center of the body-mind, roughly corresponding to the middle region of the physical heart, awakened by Grace when attention is released from the activities and conditions of the gross body, the lower mind, and the waking state. The awakening of the heart chakra is often accompanied by psychic abilities. Whether or not such abilities arise in the advanced stages of practice in the Way of the Heart, the awakening of the heart chakra is a necessary, and inevitable, occurrence in the Spiritualization of the body-mind by the Divine Life-Current.

Hridayam, Hridaya

The Sanskrit word "hridayam" means "heart". It refers not only to the physical organ but also to the True Heart, the Transcendental (and Inherently Spiritual) Divine Reality. "Hridayam" is one of Heart-Master Da's Divine Names, signifying that He Stands in, at, and as the True Heart of every being.

Hridaya-Samartha Sat-Guru

The Sanskrit word "sat" means "Truth", "Being", "Existence". The term "guru" is a composite of two contrasting words meaning "darkness" and "light". In common usage in Indian society, a guru is anyone who teaches others conventional knowledge or practical lore. A Sat-Guru, however, releases, turns, or leads living beings from darkness (non-Truth) into Light (Living Truth). Moreover, the Sat-Guru is, and lives as, the very Truth, or Condition of Being, that is Awakened in the devotee.

In the Spiritual traditions of India, the word "Samartha" (Sanskrit: "adapted", "fit", "proper", "qualified", "able", "entitled") is used to refer to that Sat-Guru who has the full Spiritual Power to overcome any obstruction to the Spiritual Process in the devotee who truly resorts to him.

However, a distinction must be made between the seventh stage, or fully Enlightened, Samartha Sat-Guru, and individuals who function in the fourth or the fifth stage of life, with siddhis (powers) of the natural energies of the body-mind or even of the Spiritual Life-Current. In Sat-Guru Da Love-Ananda's case, the Siddhis with Which He Blesses are the Expression of His seventh stage (Divine) Enlightenment, and ultimately are all born of Hridaya-Shakti or the Supreme Power of the Heart, or Reality, Itself.

The word "Hridaya" (Sanskrit: heart), which often precedes the Designation "Samartha Sat-Guru" when applied to Sat-Guru Da Love-Ananda, refers to the Very Heart, or the Transcendental (and Inherently Spiritual) Divine Reality. As applied to Heart-Master Da Love-Ananda, it points beyond all the earlier stages of life, including the sixth, to the Most Perfect Realization, in the seventh stage of life, that transcends the world, the body, the mind, and the conditional, or limited, self.

Hridaya-Vichara, Feeling-Enquiry

"Hridaya" means "Heart" in Sanskrit. The Sanskrit term "vichara" is usually translated as "enquiry", but it also connotes intense observation and unrelenting vigilance, and may also be translated as "earnest quest". "Hridaya-Vichara", then, is Sri Da Avabhasa's original term for the earnest quest to abide in Identification with the Heart (or the Feeling of Being that is the Divine Self-Condition). Unlike traditional terms such as "Atma-Vichara", "Hridaya-Vichara" does not suggest the exclusive, introverted search for the root of the essential self (atman), but points to the seventh stage Realization of the inclusive Spiritual, Transcendental, and Divine Person.

Like all meditative practices in the Way of the Heart, Hridaya-Vichara, or Feeling-Enquiry, is an extension of the primary practice of Ishta-Guru-Bhakti Yoga, which is always epitomized by feeling-Contemplation of Sri Da Avabhasa's bodily (human) Form, His Spiritual (and Always Blessing) Presence, and His Very (and Inherently Perfect) State. The twelve-part process of Feeling-Enquiry is taken up in practicing stage six of the technically "fully elaborated" form of the Way of the Heart by practitioners who are qualified for this form of the "conscious process".

intensive listening-hearing process

A practitioner of the Way of the Heart begins the intensive listening-hearing process once he or she has fulfilled the student-beginner stage. In this period of practice, the disciplines that were stabilized in the student-beginner phase are further refined, and study of the listening-hearing process itself is intensified. In the culmination of the listening phase of the Way of the Heart, to provoke the crisis of hearing, practitioners participate in regular group "considerations" that specifically address each individual's egoic limitations. By all these means, the process of self-observation and self-understanding is quickened until it becomes, by Grace, most fundamental self-understanding, or hearing.

In the final phase of this process, the practitioner goes through a period of active demonstration and stabilization of hearing, showing an obvious increase in bodily equanimity, the capability for self-transcendence, and readiness to receive Sri Da Avabhasa's Spirit-Baptism.

Ishta-Guru-Bhakti Yoga

A compound of traditional Sanskrit terms that denotes the principal Gift, Calling, and Discipline Sat-Guru Da Avabhasa Offers to all who would practice the Way of the Heart.

"Ishta" literally means "chosen", or "most beloved". "Guru", in the reference "Ishta-Guru", means specifically the Sat-Guru, the Revealer of Truth Itself (or of Being Itself). "Bhakti" means, literally, "devotion".

Ishta-Guru-Bhakti, then, is devotion to the Supreme Divine Being in the Form and through the Means of the human Sat-Guru.

"Yoga", from a Sanskrit root meaning "to yoke", "to bind together", is a path, or way, of achieving Unity with the Divine.

Japa Yoga (See Mantra Yoga and Japa Yoga.)

Jnana Samadhi

"Jnana" derives from the Sanskrit verb root "jna", literally "to know". Most individuals practicing in the sixth stage of life experience Jnana Samadhi at least once, or even frequently. Produced by the forceful withdrawal or inversion of attention from the conditional body-mind-self and its relations, Jnana Samadhi is the conditional, temporary Realization of the Transcendental Self, or Consciousness, exclusive of any perception or cognition of world, objects, relations, body, mind, or separate self-sense.

Jnana Yoga

Union with God (yoga) through Divine Wisdom (jnana).

Traditionally Jnana Yoga is associated with the non-dualistic philosophy of the Upanishads and its subsequent elaboration in Hindu Vedantic Teachings, and it is associated with practices of discriminative intelligence, self-renunciation, comprehensive self-discipline, and a fundamental orientation to Divine Liberation, or Enlightenment.

In the Way of the Heart, Jnana Yoga can be said to apply especially to practice in the sixth stage of life.

Kanya

The abbreviated Designation for a member of The Da Avabhasa Gurukula Kanyadana Kumari Order, which is the unique sacred circle of women who have consecrated themselves to the service of Sri Da Avabhasa in "true intimacy" for the sake of their Divine Self-Realization and who, by

virtue of that relationship, have the capability to serve the Spiritual growth of others by their inspiring devotional surrender to Heart-Master Da.

Karma Yoga

Union with God (yoga) through action (karma). Karma Yoga is a traditional path of uniting with the Divine through self-transcending action, or a path of service to the Divine. What makes such service an authentic religious, or Spiritual, practice is that one surrenders both one's action and all its results to God.

The original, most efficacious, and, therefore, most auspicious form of Karma Yoga is Sat-Guru-Seva, or service to the Sat-Guru. In the Way of the Heart, all practitioners practice Sat-Guru-Seva, always consciously devoting attention, the purpose or intention, the performance, and all the anticipated or otherwise actual results of any and every action to Sri Da Avabhasa.

kosha

Sanskrit: "sheath", or "body".

kumbhak

Commonly, momentary retention of the breath between exhalation and inhalation, or between inhalation and exhalation, sometimes intentionally practiced as a form of pranayama, or control of the breath. Most profoundly, temporary and total suspension of the breath while attention ascends beyond awareness of the body into states of ecstatic absorption. Both may occur spontaneously (in an easeful and blissful manner) in response to the Spiritual Presence of the Sat-Guru.

Kundalini Shakti

The traditional name for the serpent power ("kundalini" = coiled up, "shakti" = energy), or the ascending force of Spiritual Life-Energy, traditionally viewed as dormant at the bodily base, or lowermost psychic center of the body-mind, in the esoteric Yogic traditions of the fifth stage of life. It may be activated spontaneously in the devotee or by the Guru's initiation, thereafter producing all the various forms of Yogic and mystical experience.

Sri Da Avabhasa has Revealed that the Kundalini Shakti, as it is traditionally conceived, is only a partial manifestation of the universal Divine Spirit-Current. It cannot rightly be said to originate at the bodily base, since it is a continuation of the same Spirit-Current that descends in the frontal line of the body. Nor is it to be equated with the Heart-Current that Sri Da Avabhasa Speaks of and Transmits.

Kundalini Yoga (See **Nada Yoga, Kundalini Yoga, and Laya Yoga.**)

Laya Yoga (See **Nada Yoga, Kundalini Yoga, and Laya Yoga.**)

listening

"Listening" is Da Avabhasa's term for the orientation, disposition, and practice of the beginner's developmental stages of preparation and practice in the Way of the Heart. A listening devotee is someone who, in the context of his or her life of devotion, service, self-discipline, and meditation, gives his or her attention to Sri Da Avabhasa's Teaching Argument, to His Leelas (or inspirational Stories of His Life and Work), and to feeling-Contemplation of Him (primarily of His bodily human Form) for the sake of awakening most fundamental self-understanding, or hearing, on the basis of which practice may begin to develop in the Spiritual stages of life and beyond.

loka

A world or realm of experience. The term often refers to places that are subtler than the gross physical world of Earth and that can be visited only in dreams or by mystical or esoteric means.

In Sri Da Avabhasa's view, lokas are not "places" to be located somewhere in time and space but esoteric or mystical experiences of the human body-mind that may occur in the course of Yogic practice.

Mantra Yoga, Japa Yoga

Union with God (yoga) through sacred thought or word (mantra) or repetition (japa) of the sacred Name of the Divine Person or the Sat-Guru. The Spiritually imbued words (or names), phrases, or sounds are sometimes associated with various esoteric Spiritual energies, which they may, through vibration, stimulate and awaken. Most commonly, however, these sacred names and sounds are used to Invoke and Commune with the Divine Reality.

nada-bindu

A point of sound and light that may be perceived in the course of Yogic practice as attention ascends via the vertical, or spinal, line of the body-mind.

Nada Yoga, Kundalini Yoga, and Laya Yoga

Esoteric Spiritual practices associated with the stimulation and ascent of the Life-Current in the central channel.

Nada Yoga is the practice of concentration upon the internally audible Life-Current, which is heard in a range of increasingly subtle and more attractive sounds. These sounds are typically associated with the brain-mind and regions of subtlety extending above and beyond the head.

Kundalini Yoga aims at awakening latent Divine Energy, which is thought to lie dormant at the base of the perineum, so that it rises up through the spine to reunite with its ultimate source, conceived to be above the head. Typical techniques include meditative visualization and breathing exercises, but the principal means of awakening is the initiatory force of an Adept Spiritual Master.

"Laya" means "absorption", "extinction", "dissolution", or "disappearance". Laya Yoga is the most advanced stage of the ascent of the Life-Current to the point of the complete dissolution of mind through absorption in the Matrix of Light above the body, the mind, and the world.

From the beginning of His Work with His devotees, Sri Da Avabhasa has pointed out that the typical or prevailing descriptions and explanations of these processes are not founded in a true and complete understanding of the Spiritual Process. In the Nada, Kundalini, and Laya Yogas, what ascends is not merely the Life-Current (which of necessity always and already completes its full circuit in the body-mind, for otherwise the body-mind would not be sustained and enlivened by most fundamental Energy) but attention.

"Narcissus"

In Sat-Guru Da Avabhasa's Teaching-Revelation, "Narcissus" is a key symbol of un-Enlightened Man as a self-obsessed seeker, enamored of his own self-image and egoic self-consciousness. As "Narcissus", every human being constantly suffers in dilemma, contracted in every dimension of the being, recoiling from all relations and even from the fundamental condition of relationship (or relatedness) itself. In *The Knee of Listening* (p. 26), Sat-Guru Da Love-Ananda summarized His insight into "Narcissus" as the avoidance of relationship: "He is the ancient one visible in the Greek myth, who was the universally adored child of the gods, who rejected the loved-one and every form of love and relationship, who was finally condemned to the contemplation of his own image, until he suffered the fact of eternal separation and died in infinite solitude." For one who understands most profoundly, the activity of avoidance, or self-contraction, is ultimately understood to be simultaneous with the condition of relationship or relatedness itself.

Nirvikalpa Samadhi, fifth stage conditional

"Nirvikalpa" means "without form". Hence, "Nirvikalpa Samadhi" means literally "formless ecstasy". Traditionally this state is the final goal of the many schools of Yogic practice.

Fifth stage conditional Nirvikalpa Samadhi is a temporary Realization of the ascent of attention beyond all conditional manifestation into the formless Matrix of the Divine Light infinitely above the world, the body, and the mind. Like all the forms of Samadhi that may be Realized previous to Divine Self-Realization, it is a suspension of attention, produced by manipulation of attention and of the body-mind, and it is thus incapable of being maintained when attention returns, as it inevitably does, to the states of the body-mind.

In the Way of the Heart, while it is understood that fifth stage conditional Nirvikalpa Samadhi is not Divine Self-Realization, nevertheless, it is a possible, though not necessary, sign of developing Spiritual maturity.

Omega (See **Alpha and Omega**.)

"Open Eyes"

Sri Da Avabhasa's synonym for the Realization of Sahaj Samadhi, or unqualified Divine Self-Realization in the midst of arising events and conditions. The phrase "Open Eyes" graphically describes the non-exclusive, non-inward, native State of the Divinely Self-Realized Adept, who is Identi-

fied Unconditionally with the Divine Self-Reality, while also allowing whatever arises to appear in the Divine Consciousness (and spontaneously Divinely Recognizing everything that arises as only a modification of That One).

"original", "basic", and "advanced" contexts of the fourth stage of life

The "original", or beginner's, devotional context of the fourth stage of life involves the initial cultivation of devotional Heart-response to Sat-Guru Da (as Realizer and as Adept Heart-Teacher), and, thus and thereby, to the Divine Person, through consistent application to the practices of self-surrendering, self-forgetting, and self-transcending devotion, service, self-discipline, and meditation. In the Way of the Heart, this devotional course of discipline begins in the student-beginner stage (and even in the student-novice stage, of formal approach to the Way of the Heart) and extends through completion of the intensive listening-hearing phase of the Way of the Heart. It remains as the fundamental devotional context of every form and developmental stage of practice in the Way of the Heart.

The "basic" context of the fourth stage of life is true Spiritual Awakening enjoyed by practitioners who have matured beyond the beginner's stages in the Way of the Heart through emotional conversion to actively radiant love, God-Communion, and receptivity to and responsibility for Sri Da Avabhasa's Spirit-Baptism. This corresponds with the would-be-seeing stage and the first actually seeing stage in the Way of the Heart.

The "advanced" context of the fourth stage of life is characterized by the ascent of the Spirit-Current and attention toward the brain core. This is a sign of readiness for entrance into practicing stage four of the technically "fully elaborated" form of the Way of the Heart or the corresponding developmental stage of the technically "simpler" (or even "simplest") form of the Way of the Heart.

Outshined, Outshining

A term Sat-Guru Da Avabhasa uses synonymously with His term "Divine Translation", to refer to the final Demonstration of the four-phase process of Divinization in the seventh, or fully Enlightened, stage of life in the Way of the Heart. In this Event, body, mind, and world are no longer noticed, not because the Divine Consciousness has withdrawn or dissociated from manifest phenomena, but because the Ecstatic Divine Recognition of all arising phenomena (by the Divine Self, and As only modifications of Itself) has become so intense that the "Bright" Radiance of Consciousness now Outshines all such phenomena. Though this Outshining utterly transcends the mind and is therefore beyond conception, Sat-Guru Da has indicated its Process by analogy:

When you place newly made clay crocks in a furnace of great heat to dry and harden the crockery, at first the crocks become red-hot and seem to be surrounded and pervaded by a reddish glow, but they are still defined. Eventually the fire becomes white-hot, and its radiation becomes so pervasive, so bright, that you can no longer make out the separate figures of the crocks. This is the significance of Translation. (The Dreaded Gom-Boo, or the Imaginary Disease That Religion Seeks to Cure, *p. 242)*

Perfect

A technical description (with its variants, such as "Perfectly"), in Sri Da Avabhasa's Wisdom-Teaching, of the process of Divine Self-Realization in the sixth and the seventh stages of life in the Way of the Heart.

"Perfect Practice"

The "Perfect Practice" is Da Avabhasa's technical term for the discipline of the sixth stage of life and the seventh stage of life in the Way of the Heart.

Devotees who have mastered (and thus transcended the point of view of) the body-mind by fulfilling the preparatory processes of the Way of the Heart, may, by Grace, be Awakened to practice in the Domain of Consciousness Itself.

The three parts of the "Perfect Practice" are summarized by Sri Da Avabhasa in chapter 43 of *The Dawn Horse Testament* and described by Him in detail in *The Liberator (Eleutherios)* and *The Lion Sutra.*

pranic

The Sanskrit word "prana" means "life". The term is used by Sri Da Avabhasa to refer to the life-energy animating all beings and pervading everything in conditional Nature. In the human body-mind, circulation of this universal life-energy is associated with the heartbeat and the cycles of the breath. Prana is not to be equated with Spirit, Spirit-Current, or the Spiritual Presence of Sri Da Avabhasa. Even in the form of universal life-force, prana is but a conditional modification of the Spirit-Life, Which is the "Bright", or Consciousness Itself, beyond all cosmic forms.

Prayer of Remembrance

The whole-bodily exercise of Invoking Sri Da Avabhasa and surrendering body and mind into His Spiritual (and Always Blessing) Presence by means of repetition of Da Avabhasa's Principal Name, "Da". The Prayer of Remembrance (which is practiced in coordination with the cycle of the breath) is the basic devotional practice for practitioners in the Devotional Way of Faith in the third practicing stage of the technically "fully elaborated" form of the Way of the Heart. See *The Dawn Horse Testament,* chapter 22.

"Radical"

The term "Radical" derives from the Latin "radix", meaning "root", and thus it principally means "irreducible", "fundamental", or "relating to the origin". Because Sri Da Avabhasa uses "Radical" in this literal sense, it appears in quotation marks in His Wisdom-Teaching to distinguish His use of it from the popular reference to an extreme (often political) position or view.

In contrast to the evolutionary, egoic searches typically espoused by the world's religious and Spiritual traditions, the "Radical" Way of the Heart Offered by Heart-Master Da is established in the Divine Self-Condition of Reality. Every moment of its authentic practice, therefore, undermines the illusory ego at its root (the self-contraction in the heart), rendering the search not only unnecessary, but obsolete.

Raja Yoga

The "royal" Yoga, whereby the activity and formations of the mind are disciplined and made to cease. Its classical form is a practice of life that bears some resemblances to the total regime of the Way of the Heart. However, in the Way of the Heart, pacification of the mind is not achieved by any strategic, goal-oriented, ascetical, or self-willed practice that looks to achieve Enlightenment or even thoughtlessness. Rather, mind is understood to be the total psycho-physical reaction to conditionally manifested existence, and it is transcended through feeling-Contemplation of Heart-Master Da Love-Ananda.

Re-cognition

"Re-cognition", which literally means "knowing again", is Sri Da Avabhasa's term for non-verbal, heart-felt, intuitive insight into any and every arising conditional phenomenon as a form of egoic self-contraction. It is the mature form into which verbal self-Enquiry evolves in the Devotional Way of Insight in the Way of the Heart. The practitioner simply notices and tacitly "knows again", or directly understands, whatever is arising as yet another species of self-contraction, and he or she transcends or feels beyond it in Satsang with Heart-Master Da and, thus and thereby, with the Divine Person.

right side of the heart

Sri Da Avabhasa spontaneously Realized that, in the context of the body-mind, the Divine Consciousness is intuited at a psycho-physical locus in the right side of the heart. He has Revealed that this center corresponds to the sinoatrial node, or pacemaker, the source of the gross physical heartbeat in the right atrium, or upper right chamber, of the heart. Heart-Master Da affirms to His devotees that this locus is Where they will (ultimately) Find Him, or intuitively Realize Him as Consciousness, the Very Self.

The right side of the heart is to be interpreted as a locus of Consciousness only in a most paradoxical sense. Strictly speaking, the bodily heart exists in Consciousness, not vice versa. Heart-Master Da Avabhasa reminds us that, from the "Point of View" of Consciousness, there is no "where" other than Consciousness, Which transcends all psycho-physical location or place.

sadhana

Literally, "discipline", traditionally directed toward religious or Spiritual goals. In the Way of the Heart, sadhana is not action to attain Truth or any state or condition, but, rather, action that expresses a present intuition of the Divine Truth, in Satsang with Sri Da Avabhasa, the Realizer,

the Revealer, and the Revelation of that Truth.

Sahaj, Sahaj Samadhi

The Hindi word "sahaj" (Sanskrit: "sahaja") literally means "together born", or "coincident", and it is extrapolated to mean "natural", even "innate". Sri Da Avabhasa uses the term to indicate the Coincidence (in the case of Divine Self-Realization) of the Inherently Spiritual and Transcendental Divine Reality with empirical, conditional reality—the inherent, or native, and thus truly "Natural" State of Being. The "Naturalness" of Divine Self-Realization, or Sahaj Samadhi, is that it is entirely Free, unforced, and effortless, consonant with the Nature of Divine Being (Itself), Which is Self-Existing, Self-Radiant, and always already the case.

Sahaj Samadhi stands in contrast to all Samadhis previous to Perfect Divine Awakening, which always depend upon a strategic effort of the un-"Natural" self-contraction, or motion of attention, to create a temporary psycho-physical state of balance and equanimity which admits a momentary intuition of Divine Freedom.

Sat-Guru Da Love-Ananda also refers to Sahaj Samadhi as "Sahaja Nirvikalpa Samadhi" and "Inherently Perfect Nirvikalpa Samadhi", the "Natural", or "Open-Eyed", and Unconditional Realization of formless (nirvikalpa) ecstasy.

Samadhi

"Samadhi", in Sanskrit, means "placed together". It indicates concentration, equanimity, and balance, and it is traditionally used to denote various exalted states that appear in the context of esoteric meditation and Realization.

In the course of God-Realizing practice in the Company of Sri Da Avabhasa, various Samadhis may arise, the ultimate of which is Sahaj Samadhi, the unbroken Samadhi of the seventh stage of life, which must necessarily occur if the Way of the Heart is to be fulfilled.

Sat-Guru (See **Hridaya-Samartha Sat-Guru.**)

Satsang

The Sanskrit word "Satsang" literally means "true or right relationship", "the company of Truth, or of Being". In the Way of the Heart, it is the eternal relationship of mutual sacred commitment between Sri Da Avabhasa as Sat-Guru (and as the Divine Person) and each true and formally acknowledged practitioner of the Way of the Heart. Once it is consciously assumed by any practitioner, Satsang with Heart-Master Da Love-Ananda is an all-inclusive Condition, bringing Divine Grace and Blessings and sacred obligations, responsibilities, and tests into every dimension of the practitioner's life and consciousness.

sattvic

In the Hindu tradition, sattva is the principle or virtue of equilibrium and harmony, one of the three qualities, or gunas, of manifest existence (with inertia, or tamas, and motion, or rajas).

seeing

Sri Da Avabhasa's technical term for emotional conversion from the reactive emotions of the self-contracted heart to the open-hearted, Radiant Happiness that characterizes God-Love and Spiritual devotion to Him. Such true and stable emotional conversion coincides with true and stable receptivity to Sat-Guru Da's Spiritual Heart-Transmission, and these are both prerequisites to further growth in the Spiritual development of the Way of the Heart.

self-Enquiry

Self-Enquiry in the form "Avoiding relationship?", unique to the Way of the Heart, is the practice spontaneously developed by Heart-Master Da in the course of His own Ordeal of Divine Self-Realization. It is the principal technical practice in the Devotional Way of Insight in the Way of the Heart.

"sexual communion"

"Sexual communion" is the discipline of sexual intimacy engaged by practitioners in the first actually seeing stage and beyond in the Way of the Heart. It develops on the basis of sexual "conscious exercise", and it involves, like sexual "conscious exercise", the surrender of body, breath, emotion, and mind in self-transcending love of one's intimate partner. But "sexual communion", unlike sexual "conscious exercise", is a Spiritually Awakened practice of bodily surrender and Spiritual Communion with Sri Da Avabhasa.

"Sexual communion" also involves technical Yogic practices that are fully described in *The Dawn Horse Testament*, chapter 21.

sexual "conscious exercise"

Sexual "conscious exercise", practiced by sexually active devotees in the stages of practice previous to the first actually seeing stage of the Way of the Heart, is an extension of the principles of "conscious exercise" into the sphere of sexual intimacy. The practitioner engages in this regenerative sexual practice in an intentionally relaxed manner while consistently radiating heart-feeling or love to his or her intimate partner. In sexual "conscious exercise" the practitioner maintains attention, with feeling, in the sexual act itself, using the breath to aid in bodily relaxation and in the redirection of orgasmic energy into the spinal line and the whole body rather than out through the genitals.

In the first actually seeing stage of practice, sexual "conscious exercise" becomes "sexual communion". For a full technical description of sexual "conscious exercise", see *The Dawn Horse Testament*, chapter 21.

sexual conservation

This practice in the Way of the Heart involves confining one's sexual play (if one is sexually active) to fully committed intimate relationships, in nearly all cases with a single partner, preferably a practitioner of the Way of the Heart. All sexual promiscuity must be abandoned, beginning with the student-novice stage, of formal approach to the Way of the Heart.

Practitioners of the Way of the Heart engage their sexuality always in the mood of love and with sufficiently moderate frequency that sexual interest and activity are consciously inspected and naturally disciplined. Sexual conservation also involves the minimization of the discharge of sexual energy (and fluids) through the genitals.

Shakti

A Sanskrit term for the Divine Manifesting Energy, Spiritual Power, or Life-Current of the Divine Person.

Siddhi, siddhi

In Sanskrit, "siddhi" means "power", or "accomplishment". When capitalized in Heart-Master Da Love-Ananda's Wisdom-

Teaching, "Siddhi" is the Spiritual, Transcendental, and Divine Awakening-Power of the Heart that He spontaneously and effortlessly exercises as Hridaya-Samartha Sat-Guru.

The Yogic and psychic siddhis to which Sri Da Avabhasa refers in His Wisdom-Teaching are also traditionally called ordinary, or natural, siddhis. In traditional paths, such lesser siddhis are typically either sought or shunned. In the Way of the Heart, siddhis may arise as signs of the purification and enlivening of the body-mind by the Radiant Heart-Blessing of Sri Da Avabhasa. But, if and when they arise, they are neither exploited nor strategically avoided. They are simply observed, understood, and transcended, in feeling-Contemplation of Sri Da Avabhasa.

sila

A Pali Buddhist term meaning "habit", "behavior", "conduct". It connotes the restraint of outgoing energy and attention, the disposition of equanimity, or free energy and attention for the Spiritual Process.

"simpler" form of the Way of the Heart, the technically; "simplest" form of the Way of the Heart, the technically

Most individuals find, in the course of the student-beginner experiment in practice, that they are qualified for the less intensive of the two forms of the Way of the Heart that Sri Da Avabhasa Offers, and that their practice is served by a less technical form of the "conscious process". Thus, most practitioners of the Way of the Heart take up the technically "simpler" (or even "simplest") form of the Way of the Heart.

An individual practicing the technically "simpler" practice utilizes either self-Enquiry or Sat-Guru-Naama Japa.

The technically "simplest" form of the Way of the Heart is the practice of "simplest" feeling-Contemplation of Sri Da Avabhasa's bodily (human) Form, His Spiritual (and Always Blessing) Presence, and His Very (and Inherently Perfect) State, possibly accompanied by random use of Sri Da Avabhasa's Principal Name, "Da", a practice He has Given for practitioners at every developmental stage of the Way of the Heart.

Whereas the technically "simpler" (or

even "simplest") form of the Way of the Heart evolves through the same developmental stages as the technically "fully elaborated" form of the Way of the Heart, the progress is not as technically detailed in its demonstration or its description. No matter what elaborate signs of maturity may arise in the course of the technically "simpler" (or even "simplest") form of the Way of the Heart, the practitioner simply maintains the foundation practice of feeling-Contemplation of Sri Da Avabhasa by using either self-Enquiry or Sat-Guru-Naama Japa (in the technically "simpler" form of practice), or random Invocation of Sri Da Avabhasa via His Principal Name, "Da" (in the technically "simplest" form of practice), and he or she does not look to adopt technically more "elaborate" practices of the "conscious process" in response to these developmental signs.

Heart-Master Da also uses the term "'simple' practice" (as distinct from "simpler" and "simplest") to describe the practice of Contemplating Him with feeling-devotion, which is the foundation of all practice in the Way of the Heart, whatever the form of an individual's approach.

Practitioners of the Way of the Heart for whom the technically "simpler" (or even "simplest") form of the Way of the Heart is effectively self-transcending practice enter The (Free Daist) Lay Congregationist Order, where their practice is monitored by the culture of their fellow "lay congregationists" in a less intensive manner than the practice of those in the technically "fully elaborated" form of the Way of the Heart.

Spirit-Baptism

Sri Da Avabhasa's Spirit-Baptism is often felt as a Spiritual Current of life descending in the front of the body and ascending in the spinal line. Nevertheless, Sri Da Avabhasa's Spirit-Baptism is fundamentally and primarily the moveless Transmission of the Heart Itself, whereby He Rests the devotee in the Heart-Source of His Baptizing Spiritual Current and Awakens the intuition of Consciousness. As a secondary effect, the Spirit-Current Transmitted through His Great Baptism serves to purify, balance, and energize the entire body-mind of the devotee who is prepared to receive it.

Sri

Sanskrit: "flame". A term of honor and veneration, with the connotation that the one honored is "Bright" and potent with Blessing Power.

Star (See **Divine Star.**)

stages of life

Sri Da Avabhasa has described the evolutionary potential of the human individual in terms of seven stages of life.

The first three stages of life develop, respectively, the physical, emotional, and mental/volitional functions of the body-mind. The first stage begins at birth and continues for approximately five to seven years; the second stage follows, continuing until approximately the age of twelve to fourteen; and the third stage is optimally complete by the early twenties. In the case of most individuals, however, failed adaptation in the earlier stages of life means that maturity in the third stage of life takes much longer to attain, and it is usually never fulfilled, with the result that the ensuing stages of Spiritual development do not even begin.

In the Way of the Heart, however, growth in the first three stages of life unfolds in the Spiritual Company of Heart-Master Da Avabhasa and is based in the practice of feeling-Contemplation of His bodily (human) Form in devotion, service, and self-discipline in relation to His bodily (human) Form. By the Grace of this relationship to Sri Da Avabhasa, the foundation stages of life are lived and fulfilled in a self-transcending devotional disposition, or (as He describes it) "in the 'original' or beginner's devotional context of the fourth stage of life".

As the fourth stage of life continues in the Way of the Heart, heart-felt surrender to the bodily (human) Form of Sat-Guru Da Avabhasa deepens by Grace, drawing His devotee into Love-Communion with His All-Pervading Spiritual Presence. Growth in the fourth stage of life is also characterized by a Baptizing Current of Spirit-Energy that is at first felt to flow down the front of the body from above the head to the bodily base. As the fourth stage of life matures, the Spirit-Current is felt to turn about at the bodily base and ascend to the brain core.

The descending Spirit-Current releases obstructions predominantly in the waking, or bodily-based, personality, while the course of its ascent opens up the spinal line, or the subtle dimensions of psyche and mind that belong to the deeper personality, stimulating visionary and other mystical phenomena. "Conductivity" of the Spiritual Life-Current harmonizes the body-mind of Sri Da Avabhasa's devotee, awakening profound love of and devotional intimacy with Him. His devotee feels himself or herself to be the joyful servant of the Divine Person, Who is Incarnate as Sri Da Avabhasa.

In the fifth stage of life the ascending Yoga continues, and attention is concentrated in the subtle or psychic levels of awareness. The Spirit-Current is felt to penetrate the brain core and rise toward the Matrix of Light and Love-Bliss infinitely above the crown of the head, possibly culminating in the temporary experience of fifth stage conditional Nirvikalpa Samadhi, or "formless ecstasy".

In the traditional development of the sixth stage of life, attention is inverted upon the Perfectly Subjective Position of Consciousness, to the exclusion of conditional phenomena. The deliberate intention to invert attention for the sake of Realizing Transcendental Consciousness does not, however, characterize the sixth stage of life in the Way of the Heart. Rather, for devotees in the Way of the Heart, the sixth stage of life begins when the Witness-Position of Consciousness spontaneously awakens and becomes stable.

In the course of the sixth stage of life, the mechanism of attention, which is the root-action of egoity (felt as self-separation, self-contraction, or the feeling of relatedness), gradually subsides. At a felt point in the right side of the heart (corresponding to the sinoatrial node), the knot of attention dissolves and all sense of relatedness yields to the Blissful and undifferentiated Feeling of Being. The characteristic Samadhi of the sixth stage of life is the temporary and exclusive Realization of the Transcendental Self, or Consciousness Itself.

The seventh stage of life begins when Sri Da Avabhasa's devotee Awakens by Grace to Most Perfect and permanent Identification with Consciousness Itself, His Very (and Inherently Perfect) State. This is

Divine Self-Realization, the perpetual Samadhi of "Open Eyes" (Sahaj Samadhi) in which all "things" are Divinely Recognized without "difference" as merely apparent modifications of the One Self-Existing and Self-Radiant Divine Consciousness. In the course of the seventh stage of life there may be incidents of spontaneous "Moksha-Bhava Nirvikalpa Samadhi", in which psycho-physical states and phenomena do not appear to the notice, being Outshined by the "Bright" Radiance of Consciousness Itself. This Samadhi, which is the ultimate Realization of Divine Existence, culminates in Divine Translation, or the permanent Outshining of all apparent conditions in the Inherently Perfect Radiance and Love-Bliss of the Divine Self-Condition.

The seven stages of life as Revealed by Sri Da Avabhasa are not to be understood as a version of the traditional ladder of Spiritual attainment. These stages and their characteristic signs arise naturally in the course of practice for a devotee in the Way of the Heart, but the practice itself is oriented to the transcendence of the first six stages of life in the seventh stage disposition of Inherently Liberated Happiness, Granted by Grace in the Love-Blissful Spiritual Company of Heart-Master Da Avabhasa.

student-beginner

The technical term for a practitioner in the initial developmental stage of the Way of the Heart. In the course of student-beginner practice, the practitioner enters formally into an eternal bond of devotion with Sri Da Avabhasa, and, on the basis of this devotional relationship, continues the process of listening and the stabilization of the disciplines of the Way of the Heart that were begun in the student-novice stage, of preparation for the Way of the Heart.

student-novice

The technical term for an individual who is formally preparing to become a formal practitioner of the Way of the Heart. The student-novice makes a commitment to practice and is initiated into simple devotional and sacramental disciplines in formal relationship to Sri Da Avabhasa. During the student-novice stage, the individual engages in intensive study of Sri Da Avabhasa's Wisdom-Teaching and adapts to the functional, practical, relational, and cul-

tural disciplines of the Way of the Heart.

subtle (See **gross, subtle, causal.**)

"true intimacy"

"True intimacy" is Sri Da Avabhasa's technical phrase for the Spiritually based, generally long-term emotional-sexual commitment between practitioners of the Way of the Heart, in the first actually seeing stage and beyond. While the monogamous heterosexual partnership is typical of practitioners of the Way of the Heart today, as with Western society at large, Sat-Guru Da's Teaching-Revelation on this subject does not specifically address, or call for, any particular design except "true intimacy" itself. In His view, such "true intimacy" is strictly and only the mutual, self-transcending practice of the Way of the Heart, engaged under all the human, practical conditions of one or more serious, committed, emotional-sexual relationships, whatever forms it (or they) may take.

Within the Way of the Heart, no single conventional or traditional arrangement of intimate living is recommended. Some practitioners may be intimate with one another but celibate by choice. Some may be legally married, some not; some heterosexual, some homosexual. Some practice "true intimacy" without any intention to have children, while others either intend to produce children or presently have families. It is also possible that practitioners may realize "true intimacy" in a situation of multiple relationships, although Sri Da Avabhasa indicates that this is likely to be extremely rare.

For a full description of "true intimacy", see *The Dawn Horse Testament*, chapter 21.

True Heart-Master

Sri Da Avabhasa is honored by the Title "True Heart-Master" (or "Heart-Master"), because He has perfectly Realized the Heart, or the Divine Self of all beings, and because, by virtue of His Divine Self-Realization, He Transmits Heart-Awakening to others.

True Prayer

The "conscious process" of practitioners in the Devotional Way of Faith in the Way of the Heart. There are various forms of True Prayer used by practitioners

147

of the Way of the Heart according to their form of practice and developmental stage, but whatever technical form of True Prayer is being engaged at any given moment, the disposition of the practitioner is one of feeling-surrender and heart-felt Faith in the All-Accomplishing Power of Sri Da Avabhasa to Perfectly Liberate His devotee.

Witness-Consciousness

When Consciousness is free from identification with the body-mind, it takes up its natural "position" as the Witness of the body-mind.

In the Way of the Heart, the stable Realization of the Witness-Consciousness is associated with, or demonstrated via, the effortless surrender or relaxation of all seeking (and release of all motives of attention) relative to the conditional phenomena associated with the first five stages of life.

Identification with the Witness-Position, however, is not final (or Most Perfect) Realization of the Divine Self. Rather, it is the first stage of the "Perfect Practice" in the Way of the Heart, which Practice Realizes, by Heart-Master Da's Liberating Grace, complete and irreversible Identification with Consciousness Itself.

would-be-seeing stage

When hearing is fully established, a practitioner of the Way of the Heart moves into the would-be-seeing stage, which is marked by a profound Awakening to Sri Da Avabhasa's Spirit-Baptism. This period of practice should be short. The practitioner adopts a maximally conservative discipline of out-going energy (especially in the areas of social interaction and sexuality) in order to stabilize reception of Sri Da Avabhasa's Spirit-Baptism. The would-be-seeing stage is fulfilled when the practitioner has become responsible for constant devotional surrender into Sri Da Avabhasa's Spiritual Presence and is thus firmly established in the Great Grace of seeing.

yin and yang

In traditional Chinese medicine and philosophy, the cyclic dynamic of conditional Nature and the order of the universe, perceived as an alternation between active, heated, expansive, or masculine yang qualities, and passive, cooling, contractive, or feminine yin qualities.

Yoga

From the Sanskrit "yuj", meaning "to unite", usually referring to any discipline or process whereby an aspirant attempts to reunite with God. Sri Da Avabhasa acknowledges this conventional and traditional use of the term, but also, in reference to the Great Yoga of the Way of the Heart, employs it in a "Radical" sense, free of the usual implication of egoic separation and seeking.

Yoga of "Consideration"

The stages of life and developmental stages of practice previous to Divine Self-Realization in the seventh stage of life. It is the progressive outgrowing of conditional existence (or all the forms of conditional experience and conditional knowledge with which the egoic consciousness tends to be associated) from the "Point of View" and Understanding of Divine Enlightenment. Such Yoga is only preparation for the Way of the Heart, which, in Sri Da Avabhasa's Revelation of true Spiritual life, truly begins only in the seventh stage of life.

DA AVABHASA
Sri Love-Anandashram

"I Reveal The Divine Person, Who Is The Heart Itself"

A Brief Biography of the Divine World-Teacher, Da Avabhasa (The "Bright")

by Saniel Bonder

In his book *The Perennial Philosophy* (1945), Aldous Huxley, the English novelist and popularizer of Eastern and Western mysticism, spoke of the process whereby Divine Men and Women appear among us to Enlighten others:

The Logos [Divine Spirit-Word] passes out of eternity into time for no other purpose than to assist the beings, whose bodily form he takes, to pass out of time into eternity. If the Avatar's appearance upon the stage of history is enormously important, this is due to the fact that by his teaching he points out, and by his being a channel of grace and divine power he actually is, the means by which human beings may transcend the limitations of history. . . .

That men and women may be thus instructed and helped, the Godhead assumes the form of an ordinary human being, who has to earn deliverance and enlightenment in the way that is prescribed by the divine Nature of things—namely, by charity, by a total dying to self and a total, one-pointed awareness. Thus enlightened, the Avatar can reveal the way of enlightenment to others and help them actually to become what they already potentially are.[1]

1. Aldous Huxley, *The Perennial Philosophy* (New York: Harper & Row, 1970), pp. 51, 56.

A few short years before the publication of Aldous Huxley's book, just such a being had Appeared in the Western world.

Da Avabhasa was born as Franklin Albert Jones on November 3, 1939, on Long Island, New York, into an ordinary middle-class American family. For the first two years after His Birth, He continued to abide in the State of Infinite Divine Freedom and Joy that He knew prior to His physical Lifetime. Although aware of people and events around Him, He had only the barest association with the embodied state.

In the following extraordinary account, He describes the Purpose of His Birth and the mechanisms by which He "acquired" the body-mind at the age of two:

DA AVABHASA: For approximately the first two years after My Birth, I . . . allowed the gross vehicle to be gradually prepared for Me. Then, at approximately two years of age, I Spiritually descended to the region of the heart and thus established My basic association with . . . My manifested personality. . . .

This Spiritual descent into the gross body to the level of the heart occurred, when I was approximately two years old, on the basis of a sympathy or heart-response to those who were around Me at the moment. It was through this sympathetic response that I acquired the Vehicle of this body-mind.

Because I was Born to make this Submission, the decision to acquire the gross body-mind did not occur when I was two years old. The Vehicle of this body-mind had become sufficiently prepared at that point, but I had consciously decided to do this Work before I Incarnated. The descent was for the sake of the total world and all beings. I had Consciously decided to take a birth in the West. My Intention before this Birth was to take this Birth and to do My Work by complete Submission to the ordinary Western circumstance. (February 5, 1989)

No one around Da Avabhasa in His childhood sensed His Divine Nature and Destiny, so He grew up in many ways an ordinary American boy and youth of the mid-twentieth century.

But He was always aware of the Spiritual process churning in His body and mind—though He could not give it a name, or predict its ultimate result. This process often produced precocious psychic, mystical, and Yogic phenomena of a sublime (and sometimes an extremely powerful and disorienting) kind.

By His late teenage years, His original Awareness had receded into unconscious latency. At that point (while in His first year at Columbia College in New York City), He determined to do whatever was necessary to regain the Divine Freedom and Happiness He had felt during His earliest years. He devoted His next thirteen years to this quest.

His odyssey of Divine Re-Awakening was a totally spontaneous and direct exploration of every aspect of Reality, both the apparently sacred and the apparently profane. He did not know where He would find Truth and God, and He refused to be limited by the conventional sanctions of people and doctrines that, to Him, were obviously bereft of love, wisdom, and happiness.

Eventually He became an exemplary Devotee of several Spiritual Masters, including Swami Rudrananda (or "Rudi"), Swami Muktananda, and Swami Nityananda,[2] in a great Hindu lineage of extraordinary Adepts. But His own Impulse to permanently regain unqualified Divine Freedom moved His own practice and Realization beyond that which was Transmitted by

---

2.. Da Avabhasa's first Spiritual Teacher was Swami Rudrananda (1928-1973), or Albert Rudolph, known as "Rudi", who was His Teacher from 1964 to 1968, in New York City. Rudi helped Da Avabhasa prepare the foundation for the advanced and the ultimate phases of His Spiritual life. Rudi's own Teachers included the Indonesian Pak Subuh (from whom Rudi learned a basic exercise of Spiritual receptivity), Swami Muktananda Paramahansa (with whom Rudi spent many years), and Swami Nityananda (the Indian Swami who was also Swami Muktananda's Spiritual Teacher, and who was Rudi's primary Guru).

The second Teacher in Da Avabhasa's Lineage of Blessing was Swami Muktananda (1908-1982), an Adept of Kundalini Yoga who served Heart-Master Da as Spiritual Teacher during the period from 1968 to 1970.

Swami Nityananda (d. 1961), a great Yogi of South India, was Da Avabhasa's third Spiritual Teacher in His Lineage of Blessing. Although Heart-Master Da Love-Ananda did not meet Swami Nityananda in the flesh, He enjoyed Swami Nityananda's direct Spiritual Influence from the subtle plane, and He acknowledges Swami Nityananda as a direct and principal Source of Spiritual Instruction during His years with Swami Muktananda.

each of His human Teachers. Eventually, with the Blessings of Swami Nityananda, Da Avabhasa became for a time a devotee of the Divine Goddess, the infinite Source-Light or Radiant Energy appearing to Him in an archetypal female Form.[3] He enjoyed a paradoxical relationship to the Goddess as a concrete, living Personality. Such worship of the Goddess as Supreme Guru is the foundation and Spiritual Source of His Teachers' lineage, but at last Da Avabhasa's inherent Freedom Drew Him even beyond the Spiritual Blessings of the Goddess Herself, such that She ceased to function as His Guru and became, instead, His eternal Consort and Companion.

On the day following that Event, September 10, 1970, while Da Avabhasa was meditating in a small temple on the grounds of the Vedanta Society in Los Angeles, He Re-Awakened to immutable Oneness with the Consciousness, Happiness, and Love that is the Source and Substance of everyone and everything. He describes this State in His Spiritual autobiography, Written in the following year:

> . . . I remain in the unqualified state. There is a constant sensation of fullness permeating and surrounding all experiences, realms, and bodies. It is my own fullness, which is radically non-separate and includes all things. I am the form of space itself, in which all bodies, realms, and experiences occur. It is consciousness itself, which reality is your actual nature (or ultimate, and inherently perfect, Condition) now and now and now. (The Knee of Listening)

After that Great Event in the Vedanta Temple, Da Avabhasa became psychically aware of the body-minds of countless other persons and discovered that He was spontaneously "meditating" them. In time some of those individuals became associated

---

3. The Divine in Its active aspect, as the Living Divine Presence and Personality, may assume various female archetypes—the "Goddess" or "Mother Shakti" in the East, the "Virgin Mary" among Christians. Da Avabhasa first related to Her as the Virgin Mary, later as the Universal Goddess-Power. See The Divine Emergence of The World-Teacher, by Saniel Bonder, as well as Da Avabhasa's Spiritual autobiography, The Knee of Listening, for detailed accounts of this late period of Da Avabhasa's Sadhana before His Divine Re-Awakening.

with Him as His first "students" or "disciples". Finally, in April 1972, Da Avabhasa's formal Teaching Work was inaugurated when He opened a storefront Ashram in Los Angeles.

In His book *Love of the Two-Armed Form* (published in 1978), Da Avabhasa explained His method of Teaching in those years:

The method of my Teaching Work with devotees is not common, although there are many traditional or ancient precedents for it. It is not merely a subjective, internal, or even verbal activity, but a matter of intense, full, and total consideration of any specific area of experience, in living confrontation with others, until the obvious and Lawful and Divine form and practice of it becomes both clear and necessary.

. . . [Such "considerations"] always involved a period in which individuals were permitted to live through the whole matter and to be tested to the point of change.

. . . Only a "consideration" entered as such a concrete discipline can proceed all the way to its true end, which is right adaptation and freedom, or natural transcendence, relative to its functional subject. (pp. 1-2)

Whatever outward activities Da Avabhasa generated in His Teaching theatre (and they ranged from the most worldly, even apparently self-indulgent, to the most mystical and even miraculous), He was always exposing the suffering inherent in the constant activity of self-contraction, which creates the sense of a separate, un-Happy self. He likened the activity of self-contraction to the chronic, painful clenching of a fist, but at every level of body, mind, and heart. And He patiently demonstrated that those who wish to understand and transcend the activity of self-contraction and thereby open up to the All-Pervading Life-Power of Reality must submit to an all-encompassing discipline.

Even in the midst of "consideration" and Teaching theatre, Da Avabhasa often reminded His devotees that He could not continue indefinitely to engage a method of Teaching that

required Him to take on the human likeness of His devotees—
that is, to conduct Himself among them in a sympathetic, broth-
erly way, often adopting their habits of speech and action, in
order to allow them to become sympathetically Attracted to
Him. In early 1978 He warned that at some point it would
become impossible for Him to "hold on to the body-mind" and
forestall "release into Inherently Perfect Energy". At last, that
moment arrived in the pre-dawn darkness of January 11, 1986,
at His Hermitage Ashram in Fiji. His devotees' failure to transcend
the mind and habits of egoity and to become God-Realizing
practitioners of His Way of the Heart had brought Him to the
point of despair. In a sudden crisis of anguish, He entered into
an extraordinary death-like Yogic state.

When He returned to bodily awareness some moments
later, Da Avabhasa had spontaneously and completely relinquished the Impulse to Identify with others in order to reflect
their egoity to them. The necessity and the ability to Teach in
that unique manner had simply dissolved.

And, with that dissolution of His persona as Teacher, Da
Avabhasa had fully "Emerged" as The Divine Self in bodily
(human) Form. The change marked such an immense Spiritual
descent and intensification that He later said of it, "In a sense
that Event was My Birth Day." He has indicated that this Event,
the initiation of His Divine Emergence, marks an even greater
moment than His Re-Awakening in September 1970.

It was at this time that "Da Free John" (as He was then
known) took the Name "Da Love-Ananda Hridayam". "Love-
Ananda", a Name that had been Given to Him in 1969 by
Swami Muktananda, means "Inherent Love-Bliss", and "Hridayam"
means "the Heart". His principal Name, "Da", meaning "the
One Who Gives", had been Revealed to Him some years earlier
in vision and by other Spiritual means. Thus, the Name "Da
Love-Ananda Hridayam" indicates that He is the Divine Giver of
the Inherent Love-Bliss that is the Heart Itself.

Five years later, on April 30, 1991, this Great Adept Revealed
a new Name—"Da Avabhasa (The 'Bright')"—in response to His

devotees' confessed acknowledgements of His Radiant, bodily Revelation of God.

"Avabhasa", in Sanskrit, has a rich range of associations. As a noun it means "brightness", "appearance", "manifestation", "splendor", "lustre", "light", "knowledge". As a verb it may be interpreted as "shining toward", "shining down", "showing oneself". The Name "Da Avabhasa", then, praises the Mystery of Da, the Divine Being, "Brightly" Appearing as Man. It points to His Divine Emergence and the ever-growing Radiance of His bodily (human) Form that is apparent to all who have been Graced to see Him particularly since the Great Event of 1986.

The Name "Da Avabhasa" also points to His role as Sat-Guru—meaning One who brings the light of Truth into the darkness of the human world.

The "Bright", as Da Avabhasa tells us in *The Knee of Listening,* was, in fact, His own earliest description of the sublime Condition He enjoyed at Birth. He speaks of this Condition as "an incredible sense of joy, light, and freedom". He was, He says, "a radiant form, a source of energy, bliss, and light. . . . the power of Reality, a direct enjoyment and communication. . . . the Heart who lightens the mind and all things." Even His entire life, as He once said, has been "an adventure and unfolding in the 'Bright'", the Radiance, Bliss, and Love of the God-State.

Da Avabhasa is not merely an extraordinary Teacher. He is not merely a man of uncommonly profound Spiritual experience who has managed to put together a remarkably comprehensive and insightful Teaching, and who can transmit vivid Spiritual experiences. He is, rather, a Realizer and Transmitter of the Source of all Being. This is what His devotees mean when we refer to Him as "Divine World-Teacher". The phrase "World-Teacher" comes from Sanskrit terms meaning "One Who Liberates everything that moves"—that is, all things and beings. Da Avabhasa's Wisdom-Teaching is a complete Revelation of the ultimate Wisdom relative to every aspect of existence and every stage of our possible growth and Realization. And His Grace is universally active and universally available.

All this has been confirmed to me through the vision Given in His physical Company—a whole bodily intuition that I have felt and seen face to face with Him. It is a deep and life-changing Revelation that has also been enjoyed by all kinds of ordinary people from all over the world, a vision of Him in physical Form that also Reveals the Divine Self and Love-Bliss of our very Being.

Da Avabhasa has come into this world to restore Wisdom and the Way of Truth, and to Bless all beings toward Divine Freedom, Happiness, Enlightenment, and Love. He excludes absolutely no one from His Blessing and His Help. As the Divine Self of all, He continuously Gives His Benediction to everyone, everywhere.

To learn more about this sacred opportunity, please see the invitation on the following pages.

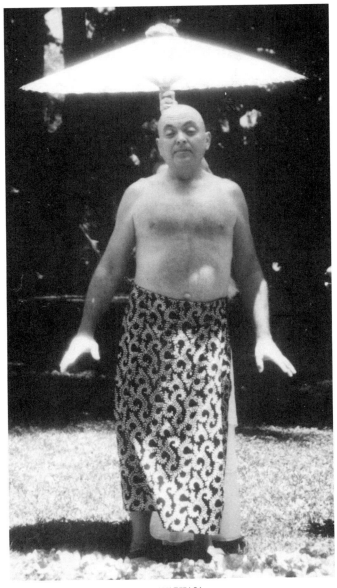

DA AVABHASA
Sri Love-Anandashram

"A Unique Advantage to Mankind"

An Invitation to a Direct Relationship with Da Avabhasa

by Carolyn Lee

The human Spiritual Master is an agent to the advantage of those in like form. When one enters into right relationship with a Spiritual Master, changes happen in the literal physics of one's existence. It is not just a matter of ideas. I am talking about transformations at the level of energy, at the level of the higher light of physics, at the level of mind beyond the physical limitations that people now presume, at the level of the absolute Speed of ultimate Light. The transforming process is enacted in devotees, duplicated in them in and through that Living Company. It is not a matter of conceptual symbolisms or emotional attachment to some extraordinary person. It is real physics. And it is to the advantage of people when someone among them has gone through the whole cycle of Transformation, because they can then make use of the Offering of that Process, that Company.

Da Avabhasa
Scientific Proof of the Existence of God Will Soon Be
Announced by the White House!

If you feel a heart-response to what you have read in this book, or if you simply feel moved to find out more about Da Avabhasa and the Way of the Heart, we invite you to explore the Sacred Literature of Da Avabhasa.

To focus your exploration we wish to draw your attention here to four of our publications by and about Da Avabhasa that will be especially useful introductions or overviews of the Way of the Heart. (More complete descriptions of these publications can be found on pages 175-87.)

Most important for your ongoing study are Da Avabhasa's "Source-Texts" or Scriptures, conclusively summarizing His Word of Instruction. We recommend that you begin with *THE LOVE-ANANDA GITA (The Wisdom-Song Of Non-Separateness)* The "Simple" Revelation-Book Of Da Avabhasa (The Divine World-Teacher and True Heart-Master, Da Love-Ananda Hridayam).

You will also find very helpful (and may wish to distribute to friends) an introductory booklet, *YOUR SUFFERING IS YOUR OWN ACTIVITY: Is This Good News or Bad News?* by Kanya Samatva Suprithi. The author is a devotee engaged in the ultimate practice of the Way of the Heart who speaks from profound personal experience. She summarizes Da Avabhasa's fundamental Argument about seeking and Happiness in simple and accessible terms.

THE DIVINE EMERGENCE OF THE WORLD-TEACHER: The Realization, the Revelation, and the Revealing Ordeal of Da Avabhasa is a full-length "Biographical Celebration" of Da Avabhasa's Life and Work to date, by Saniel Bonder, a long-time practitioner of the Way of the Heart.

DIVINE DISTRACTION: A Guide to the Guru-Devotee Relationship, the Supreme Means of God-Realization, as Fully Revealed for the First Time by The Divine World-Teacher and True Heart-Master, Sri Da Avabhasa (The "Bright") is an introduction to the Guru-devotee relationship. It was written by James Steinberg, another long-time devotee of Da Avabhasa.

There are thousands of people all over the world today reading Da Avabhasa's books, and some people have been reading them for a long time. But reading, while necessary and helpful, will only take you so far on its own. Once you acknowledge the greatness—the Truth—of Da Avabhasa's Wisdom-Revelation, it begins to require something of you.

Da Avabhasa's literature is a Divine Gift, not to be treated casually. "Such Transmissions of Teaching do not occur arbitrarily," as Da Avabhasa says. "They are part of the higher scale of activity in the cosmos." Thus, it is only when you begin to participate in the practice and the sacred culture Da Avabhasa Offers that you really find out what it is about—Spiritual transformation and God-Realization never happened in an armchair!

Therefore, in addition to reading, we urge you to attend the lectures, seminars, courses, and other events that our missionary institution, Da Avabhasa International, makes available to the public in your area. At these events you will have the opportunity to see videotapes of Da Avabhasa and to meet practitioners of the Way of the Heart who can speak to you about His Wisdom and tell you Leelas of their own relationship with Him. You can also participate in a Da Avabhasa International Study Group in your area, joining others for a weekly evening meeting of recitations of Da Avabhasa's Word and listening to or viewing audio-visual presentations about Da Avabhasa and the Way of the Heart.

All of this can lead to a deepening intuition of Who He Is and a deepening impulse to practice the Way of the Heart as His devotee.

Carol Mason, who lives in northern California, describes the process that brought her to the point of entering into a formal relationship with Da Avabhasa:

For over thirty years I sought Enlightenment. But despite profound Zen realizations and unusual Kundalini experiences, despite my teachers' acknowledgements of my attainment and good understanding, I realized that fundamentally I had not changed. I saw the failure of my search, and I despaired.

Then I read The Knee of Listening, *Da Avabhasa's Spiritual autobiography, and I began to have dreams of Him. In the dreams, He Instructed me, He laughed, He gave Talks at which many people gathered. He sat silently in Darshan and escorted me to subtle realms. I was able to feel Him as a Spiritual Friend and Teacher during the day. I found through study that His Wisdom-Teaching had the power of mantra. The Truth of it became alive in me.*

Several months after I read The Knee of Listening *I saw a videotape of Da Avabhasa made during His Teaching years. At first sighting I acknowledged Him to be the True Master of Liberation, the One Whom all the world's religions await. I bowed down. I celebrated Him with thoughts of praise and soon He was all I thought about, all I wanted to talk about. For an entire year He was always available to me, but suddenly, one day, I no longer experienced Him, no longer felt His Influence or received His Instruction. Then one final time I heard His Voice: "Now, what will* you *do?"*

Realizing I must now approach Him in the traditional devotional manner, I became a formal participant in Da Avabhasa International and soon thereafter I became a student-novice, taking on the studies, disciplines, and meditation practices required of a novice, and consciously cultivating my devotional relationship with my Heart-Teacher. Even during this rudimentary stage of practice, Da Avabhasa has, on occasion, Blessed me with Heart-Bliss, with the purification of my karmic tendencies, and with a deepening sense of His Divine Form. I am ever grateful.

You should know that all of this has taken place without Carol's ever meeting Da Avabhasa in the flesh. The same is true for thousands of others around the world, who, like Carol, are being drawn spontaneously into a sacred relationship with Da Avabhasa and are taking steps to honor that relationship in a formal way.

When you enter into formal involvement with Da Avabhasa International, you are expressing your intention to become a practitioner of the Way of the Heart as a formally acknowledged member of The Free Daist Communion. You are encouraged to apply immediately to become a **student-novice**, and so take on in rudimentary form the range of devotional practices and disciplines that Da Avabhasa Offers to Free Daist practitioners. If you need to spend a month or two preparing to take up the practices of a student-novice, then you can become a **student** or a **tithing member** first. Students and tithing members engage a specific practice based on study and service, as I will describe in a moment. They offer an initial donation on entering Da Avabhasa International and, in addition, tithing members contribute 10% of their net monthly income in support of The Free Daist Communion.

If you are moved by the importance of Da Avabhasa's Work and would like to show your gratitude for His Presence in the world without becoming a practitioner of the Way of the Heart (at least for the time being), then you may wish to become a Friend of The Free Daist Communion. A Friend is essentially a patron, someone who accepts a level of responsibility for funding the missionary services of The Free Daist Communion and

also for supporting the Treasures of Da Avabhasa's Work—principally His personal Circumstance and His Hermitage Ashram, in Fiji. Some Friends contribute a minimum fixed fee each year, others tithe regularly, and some are able to offer major financial support. Being a Friend is a particular form of sadhana (or life-practice)—a very honorable way of associating with Da Avabhasa. At the same time, Friends are always invited and encouraged to take the further step of preparing to become a formal practitioner of the Way of the Heart.

For students, tithing members, and student-novices, who have already decided to practice the Way of the Heart, an intensive study of Da Avabhasa's Instruction is essential at the beginning of practice. As you do this day by day, in a guided way (using the study courses provided), you will be astonished at how your understanding of yourself and your response to Da Avabhasa will deepen and grow. I began my formal association with the practice as a correspondent living hundreds of miles from the closest gathering of devotees, and so study was my lifeline and the most exciting part of my life. Guided study, more than anything else, clarified my intention to practice, instructed me in every aspect of my life, and placed my relationship to Da Avabhasa on a firm foundation.

Study, among other things, is a discipline of attention. Service is a more bodily-based discipline, but it is no different in principle. It is a way of actively bringing your energy and attention to Da Avabhasa. The discipline of service within the sphere of an Adept's Blessing is not about making yourself useful. It is a sacred matter. Traditionally the discipline of service was called "Karma Yoga", and it was understood to encompass the whole of one's life. Karma Yoga was the basic practice given to beginners, and especially to householders who had many obligations in the world. It was the great practice of devoting one's actions to God, of contemplating the Divine in the midst of all activity.

As a student or a tithing member, you will be invited to spend at least a few hours each week in some form of direct service to Da Avabhasa or the community of practitioners of the

**Students and tithing members engage a specific practice
based on study and service**

The Mountain Of Attention Sanctuary

Way of the Heart. You may find yourself cleaning your local community bookstore or helping with the missionary work by putting up posters for our public events. If you have special skills in any area, we of Da Avabhasa International will help you find ways to use those skills to the maximum. For example, one participant in Da Avabhasa International, who happens to be an architect and university professor, has recently begun to supervise the designing of a community Ashram for devotees in Lake County, California, near The Mountain Of Attention Sanctuary.

Whatever your form of service at any time, whether it is something you like doing or something you would not personally choose, the secret is to live it as a self-transcending gesture of devotion to Da Avabhasa. I recall with some amusement my first encounter with the discipline of service and all the resistance I felt. It was a wintry weekend early in 1986. I had made the journey to London from Ireland at considerable expense just to spend the weekend with devotees there. No sooner had I arrived from the airport than I found myself with a paint-scraper in one hand and sandpaper in the other. Everyone was busy around the clock renovating the newly-acquired mission-ary house associated with the London regional center. I still had on my professional clothes, I was developing a very uncomfort-able sore throat, and I had been so tired before leaving Ireland that my friends there had begged me not to go.

Needless to say, I very nearly turned around and went back to the airport. But somehow I didn't. My dismay was so acute that it was <u>interesting</u> to me. I wanted to see what would happen if I actually stayed and participated. Would I die or develop bronchial pneumonia? And so I scraped, painted, cleaned, put up wallpaper with everyone else. For the first hour or two the only way I was able to stick at it was by con-centrating with fierce intention on Da Avabhasa and remember-ing His Instruction about Happiness ("You cannot <u>become</u> Happy, you can only <u>be</u> Happy"). This was the most intense moment of practice I had ever been through, and it bore fruit. As the evening wore on I ceased to be so concerned about myself. There was a lot of laughter, and it did not seem to mat-ter that I hardly knew anyone when I walked in. By the time I emerged from the plaster dust well after midnight, I was simply happy. I still had a sore throat, but by the next morning it was almost gone. And I was not tired anymore. I felt uncommonly alive, focused, and alert. All I could think about was Da Avabhasa, how attractive He is, so attractive that I was ready to transcend myself in response to Him and accomplish things I would never have dreamed of attempting otherwise.

Becoming a student-novice is a crucial turning point, because it is the moment of committing yourself unequivocally to Da Avabhasa in the eternal sacred bond of the Guru-devotee relationship.

As a student-novice of Da Avabhasa International, and,

. . . you will gradually adapt to further disciplines relative to meditation, sacramental worship, exercise, diet and health, sexuality, child-rearing, cooperative community, right use of money and energy, and other aspects of daily living. . . . All of the disciplines simply support the primary practice of Free Daism, which is Satsang (the "Company of Truth"), or the cultivation of the relationship to Da Avabhasa.

later, as a formally acknowledged practitioner of The Free Daist Communion, you will gradually adapt to further disciplines relative to meditation, sacramental worship, exercise, diet and health, sexuality, child-rearing, cooperative community (including formal membership in The Free Daist Community Organization), right use of money and energy, and other aspects of daily living. These practices are necessary to develop bodily equanimity, free attention, and the capability for self-transcendence, without which nothing great can be Realized. But they are not an end in themselves. All of the disciplines simply support the primary practice of Free Daism, which is Satsang (the "Company of Truth"), or the cultivation of the relationship to Da Avabhasa. Devotees are Called to Remember Da Avabhasa at all times, not merely to think about Him, but to locate the <u>feeling</u> of Him, the feeling-sense of His Being that He Grants you when you sit in front of Him and regard His bodily (human) Form. While the great opportunity to come into Da Avabhasa's physical Company occurs only occasionally for most of His devotees, you can find the same feeling by His Grace in any moment of heart-felt resort to Him. Turning to His picture, Remembering His Image in the mind's eye, listening to recitations of His Word or Stories of His Work—all these and other means are potent aids to feeling-Contemplation of Him.

By reading in the tradition of Guru-devotion (which you will begin to do formally as a student-novice), by studying Da Avabhasa's own Wisdom-Teaching about the practice of feeling-Contemplation of Him, and especially by doing the practice of it according to His specific Instructions, you will discover why this form of sacred Remembrance is so potent, so revealing, and so Liberating. For the devotee, feeling-Contemplation becomes a literal life-support as basic as food and rest.

The best goad to practice is the possibility of coming into the physical Company of Sri Da Avabhasa. I was Graced to see Him bodily very soon after I committed myself to formal practice, and that sighting Revealed to me beyond any doubt that Da Avabhasa is Who He says He is, "The Realizer, The Revealer, and The Revelation Of The Divine Person". There is no greater Blessing than to come into the Company of His bodily (human) Form and feel His Regard face to face. To Contemplate the Divine Person, Compassionately Appearing in a human body, is an unfathomable, heart-breaking Mystery.

Whoever you are, wherever you live, whatever your apparent liabilities, this Grace could be yours in a relatively short period of time, if you fulfill the requirements of a student-novice and then rightly prepare yourself as a formally acknowledged practitioner of the Way of the Heart. The place you are most likely to see Da Avabhasa is Sri Love-Anandashram, His Hermitage Sanctuary, in Fiji, and where He Offers retreats to qualified practitioners from all over the world.

Over the years Da Avabhasa has often pointed out in a vivid, humorous fashion that whoever is serious about practice in His Company is going to have to go through a fiery ordeal.

Da Avabhasa with retreatants at Sri Love-Anandashram

The Way of the Heart is the Way of Grace, certainly, but it is not, as He has said, a "bliss-ride". This is how it has always been in the company of a genuine Adept, because there are Divine Laws involved in the Spiritual process, and the principal Law is the Law of sacrifice, the mutual sacrifice constantly enacted between the Guru and the devotee. The Guru Transmits the Divine Siddhi (or Power of Liberation), and the devotee renounces the egoic self, granting all feeling and attention, more and more profoundly, to the Guru.

The members of The Da Avabhasa Gurukula Kanyadana Kumari Order, four renunciate women practitioners who live and serve in Da Avabhasa's intimate sphere, have fulfilled this Ordeal of Guru-devotion to an extraordinary degree. Every practitioner who comes in contact with the Kanyas is deeply impressed by their radiant Happiness in the midst of all circumstances and by the profundity of their transformation as human beings. The Kanyas are a great sign of the Truth of Da Avabhasa's Wisdom and the effectiveness of His Work.

The magnitude of the Gift Da Avabhasa Brings to humanity is also being Revealed through the developing sacred culture of Free Daism. If you decide to participate in Da Avabhasa International and to proceed from there to become a formally

The Da Avabhasa Gurukula Kanyadana Kumari Order

acknowledged practitioner of the Way of the Heart, you will be collaborating in a unique experiment—the founding of a culture and a community whose sacred practice is always founded in direct enjoyment of the Happiness of the seventh stage of life, as Transmitted by a living, seventh stage Realizer, the Divine World-Teacher, Da Avabhasa.

How often has such a Being as Da Avabhasa Appeared? If such a One is here now, is there anything more worth doing than to enter into His Company? He is addressing you personally when He says:

DA AVABHASA: Physical embodiment has the purpose of Enlightenment, the purpose of purification. . . . If you will receive My Teaching-Revelation, if you will "consider" it, if you will become responsive, then you become capable of making use of this lifetime for the purpose it inherently can serve. . . . You must submit the body-mind to the Great Purpose. . . . That is what I am Calling you to do. Accept the Dharma, the Law, inherent in your birth, the purpose that is inherent in your birth. Take up the Way of the Heart in My Company. (August 15, 1988)

If you are feeling the urge to move beyond your present level of human growth and are interested in what Da Avabhasa is Offering you, contact us at one of the addresses listed below. We will be happy to send you a free brochure on the forms of participation available to you. We invite you to enter into this sacred relationship with Da Avabhasa, and be tempered and opened in God by His Grace. We look forward to hearing from you.

Correspondence Department

THE FREE DAIST COMMUNION
P.O. Box 3680
Clearlake, California 95422 USA
Phone: (707) 928-4936

THE REGIONAL CENTERS OF
THE FREE DAIST COMMUNION

UNITED STATES
NORTHERN CALIFORNIA
The Free Daist Communion
740 Adrian Way
San Rafael, CA 94903
415-492-0930
415-492-0216

NORTHWEST USA
The Free Daist Communion
7214 Woodlawn Ave NE
Seattle, WA 98115
206-691-6818
206-522-2298

SOUTHWEST USA
The Free Daist Communion
11454 Washington Blvd.
Los Angeles, CA 90066
213-391-8344

NORTHEAST USA
The Free Daist Communion
263 Washington St.
Wellesley, MA 02181
617-237-8827
617-654-1538

SOUTHEAST USA
The Free Daist Communion
10301 South Glen Rd.
Potomac, MD 20875
301-983-0291

HAWAII
The Free Daist Communion
P.O. Box 3111
Lihue, HI 96766
808-822-3386
808-822-0216

AUSTRALIA
Da Avabhasa Ashram
Myers Creek Rd.
Box 562
Healesville, Victoria 3777
Australia
3-4177-069

EASTERN CANADA
The Free Daist Communion
75 Blantyre Ave.
Scarborough, Ontario M1N 2RS
Canada
416-698-0305

THE NETHERLANDS
Da Avabhasa Ashram
Annendaalderweg 10
6105 At Maria Hoop
The Netherlands
4743-1281
4743-1872

NEW ZEALAND
The Free Daist Communion
61 Opanuku Rd.
Box 3185 Auckland
New Zealand
814-9272

THE UNITED KINGDOM
AND IRELAND
Da Avabhasa Ashram
Tasburgh Hall
Lower Tasburgh
Norwich NR1 5LT
England
441-883-1827

"An Exquisite Manual for Transformation"

The Sacred Literature of Da Avabhasa (The "Bright")

eart-Master Da Love-Ananda provides a way in which Oneness may be experienced by anyone who is bold enough to follow his teachings. It is important to understand that his vision is neither Eastern nor Western, but it is the eternal spiritual pulse of the Great Wisdom which knows no cultural, temporal, or geographical locus; it represents the apex of awareness of our species.

Larry Dossey, M.D.
author, *Space, Time, and Medicine* and *Beyond Illness*

he teachings of Heart-Master Da, embodied in an extraordinary collection of writings, provide an exquisite manual for transformation. . . . I feel at the most profound depth of my being that his work will be crucial to an evolution toward full-humanness.

Barbara Marx Hubbard
author, *The Evolutionary Journey*

Do you hunger for Spiritual Truth?

Do you long to know precisely why everything you seek, and everything you hold on to, never seems to give you lasting fulfillment?

Do you wish to see the whole process of Spiritual Awakening explained, and all the conflicting paths and doctrines of humanity clarified, by an all-illuminating Revelation of sacred understanding?

Are you ready for Wisdom that shows you exactly how you unconsciously cut yourself off from the Divine Reality—and exactly how to reconnect, and to always participate consciously in that Reality, with every breath, in all relationships, in all action and meditation, even to the degree of Perfect Divine Self-Realization?

If your answer to any of these questions, or all of them, is "yes", then you need seek no further. We invite you to explore the Sacred Literature of Da Avabhasa.

175

SOURCE LITERATURE

THE LOVE-ANANDA GITA

*(THE WISDOM-SONG OF
NON-SEPARATENESS)*
*The "Simple" Revelation-Book Of Da
Kalki (The Divine World-Teacher
and True Heart-Master,
Da Love-Ananda Hridayam)*

   The Love-Ananda Gita is Da
Avabhasa's quintessential Revelation of His
Way of the Heart, containing His basic
Instructions on the fundamental practice
of Satsang, or feeling-Contemplation of
His bodily (human) Form, His Spiritual
(and Always Blessing) Presence, and His
Very (and Inherently Perfect) State of Free
Being. The most basic Source-Text of His
entire Word of Confession and Instruction.
(The next edition of *The Love-Ananda
Gita* will be published with the following
attribution: *The "Simple" Revelation-Book
of The Divine World-Teacher and True
Heart-Master, Da Avabhasa [The "Bright"].)*
Standard Edition
$34.95 cloth, $19.95 paper

THE DAWN HORSE TESTAMENT

*The "Testament Of Secrets"
Of The Divine World-Teacher
and True Heart-Master,
Da Avabhasa (The "Bright")*

   In this monumental text of over
800 pages (a substantial revision of the
original Work published in 1985), Da
Avabhasa Reveals the Mysteries and
devotional Secrets of every practice and
developmental stage of the Way of the
Heart. Ken Wilber, renowned scholar of
Eastern and Western psychology and
religion, was moved to write:

   The Dawn Horse Testament *is the
most ecstatic, most profound, most
complete, most radical, and most
comprehensive <u>single</u> spiritual text ever
to be penned and confessed by the
Human-Transcendental Spirit.*
New Standard Edition (forthcoming,
mid-1991)

THE DA UPANISHAD

*THE SHORT DISCOURSES
ON self-RENUNCIATION,
GOD-REALIZATION, AND THE
ILLUSION OF RELATEDNESS*

Da Avabhasa's most concise Instruction relative to the forms of the Way of the Heart described in *The Dawn Horse Testament,* emphasizing the non-strategic, non-ascetical practice of renunciation in the Way of the Heart. (*The Da Upanishad* is an enlarged and updated edition of Da Avabhasa's Work formerly titled *The Illusion Of Relatedness.* The next edition will be titled *The Da Avabhasa Upanishad.*) Standard Edition
$19.95 paper

THE ego-"I" is THE ILLUSION OF RELATEDNESS

Published here in book form, this central Essay from *The Da Avabhasa Upanishad* is an indispensable introduction to the esoteric Wisdom-Instruction of the Divine World-Teacher of our time. It includes Da Avabhasa's utterly extraordinary commentaries on dietary and sexual Yoga, His Divinely Enlightened secrets on how to responsibly master and transcend all of the psycho-physical "sheaths" or bodies, and passage after passage that exposes the very core of our suffering, the illusion of relatedness.
$8.95 paper

THE BASKET OF TOLERANCE

*A GUIDE TO PERFECT
UNDERSTANDING OF THE ONE AND
GREAT TRADITION OF MANKIND*

Never before in history has it been possible for a seventh stage Adept to Give the world such a Gift: a comprehensive bibliography (listing more than 2,500 publications) of the world's historical traditions of truly human culture, practical self-discipline, perennial religion, universal religious mysticism, "esoteric" (but now openly communicated) Spirituality, Transcendental Wisdom, and Perfect (or Divine) Enlightenment, compiled, presented, and extensively annotated by Da Avabhasa Himself. The summary of His Instruction on the Great Tradition of human Wisdom and the Sacred ordeal of Spiritual practice and Realization.
New Standard Edition (forthcoming, late 1991)

THE LION SUTRA

*(ON PERFECT TRANSCENDENCE
OF THE PRIMAL ACT, WHICH IS
THE ego-"I", THE self-CONTRACTION,
OR attention itself, AND ALL THE
ILLUSIONS OF SEPARATION,
OTHERNESS, RELATEDNESS,
AND "DIFFERENCE")
The "Perfect" Revelation-Book Of
The Divine World-Teacher and
True Heart-Master, Da Avabhasa
(The "Bright")*

A poetic Exposition of the "Perfect Practice" of the Way of the Heart—the final stages of Transcendental, Inherently Spiritual, and Divine Self-Realization. Of all Da Avabhasa's Works, *The Lion Sutra* is the most concentrated Call and Instruction to Realize the Consciousness that Stands prior to body, mind, individual self, and objective world. (First published in 1986 under the title *Love-Ananda Gita*.) New Standard Edition (forthcoming, mid-1991)

THE LIBERATOR (ELEUTHERIOS)

AN EPITOME OF PERFECT WISDOM AND THE "PERFECT PRACTICE"

In compelling, lucid prose, Da Avabhasa distills the essence of the ultimate processes leading to Divine Self-Realization in the Way of the Heart—the "Perfect Practice", which involves the direct transcendence of all experience via identification with Consciousness Itself, through feeling-Contemplation of His Form, His Presence, and (most crucial in these stages of practice) His infinite State. New Standard Edition (forthcoming, mid-1991)

INTRODUCTORY TEXTS

FREE DAISM

THE ETERNAL, ANCIENT, AND NEW RELIGION OF GOD-REALIZATION
by *Richard Schorske*

Addressed to new readers and written in a highly accessible style, *Free Daism* thoroughly introduces Da Avabhasa and the sacred orders of His most exemplary devotees, the stages and disciplines of the Way of the Heart, and the unique features of the institution, the sacred devotional culture, and the worldwide community of His devotees.
(forthcoming, late 1991)

LOVE OF THE GOD-MAN

A COMPREHENSIVE GUIDE TO THE TRADITIONAL AND TIME-HONORED GURU-DEVOTEE RELATIONSHIP, THE SUPREME MEANS OF GOD-REALIZATION, AS FULLY REVEALED FOR THE FIRST TIME BY THE DIVINE WORLD-TEACHER AND TRUE HEART-MASTER, DA AVABHASA (THE "BRIGHT")
by *James Steinberg*

An extensive discussion of the profound laws and virtues of the Guru-devotee relationship as practiced in the Way of the Heart. Nowhere else in the literature of sacred life does such an encyclopedic treatment of the Guru-devotee relationship exist. *Love of the God-Man* is an inexhaustible resource, full of Da Avabhasa's Wisdom and His Leelas (inspiring stories) and many stories from the Great Tradition. Second Edition (forthcoming, mid-1991)

DIVINE DISTRACTION

A GUIDE TO THE GURU-DEVOTEE RELATIONSHIP, THE SUPREME MEANS OF GOD-REALIZATION, AS FULLY REVEALED FOR THE FIRST TIME BY THE DIVINE WORLD-TEACHER AND TRUE HEART-MASTER, DA AVABHASA (THE "BRIGHT")
by *James Steinberg*

Presented by a long-time devotee of Da Avabhasa, this shorter version of *Love of the God-Man* describes, illustrates, and extols the Guru-devotee relationship. *Divine Distraction* features compelling stories of Da Avabhasa's Work with His devotees, and illuminating

passages from His Wisdom-Teaching, along with instruction and stories from great Masters and disciples in the world's religious and Spiritual traditions.
(forthcoming, mid-1991)

FEELING WITHOUT LIMITATION
AWAKENING TO THE TRUTH BEYOND FEAR, SORROW, AND ANGER

A brief introductory volume featuring a Discourse from Da Avabhasa's Teaching years that presents in simplest terms His fundamental Argument about human suffering, seeking, and freedom. Also includes remarkable Leelas and testimonies by three devotees.
$4.95 paper

YOUR SUFFERING IS YOUR OWN ACTIVITY
IS THIS GOOD NEWS OR BAD NEWS?
by Kanya Samatva Suprithi

A gem of a booklet by one of the four most mature practitioners of the Way of the Heart, a woman who has entered the sixth stage of life through Da Avabhasa's Grace. Kanya Suprithi presents here a very readable summary of Da Avabhasa's basic Arguments about seeking and Happiness, and she includes some of her own story as a Daist practitioner. An excellent and very concise introduction to Da Avabhasa and His Work.
$1.95 paper

AVADHOOTS, MAD LAMAS, AND FOOLS
by James Steinberg

A brief and lively account of the "Crazy Wisdom" style of sacred Instruction employed by Adepts in many traditions, times, and cultures, including Leelas of Da Avabhasa's Teaching years and His Divine Emergence Work.
(forthcoming, mid-1991)

THE WISDOM-LITERATURE OF DA AVABHASA'S TEACHING WORK

THE KNEE OF LISTENING

THE EARLY LIFE AND EARLIEST "RADICAL" SPIRITUAL TEACHINGS OF THE DIVINE WORLD-TEACHER AND TRUE HEART-MASTER, DA AVABHASA (THE "BRIGHT")

VOLUME I

THE LIFE OF UNDERSTANDING

Da Avabhasa's autobiographical record of the very human—as well as Spiritual, Transcendental, and Divine—Ordeal of His Illumined birth and His boyhood in America, His Spiritual insights, practice, and growth as a Devotee of great modern Yogic Adepts, and His Divine Re-Awakening or Enlightenment.
New Standard Edition (forthcoming, 1992)

VOLUME II

THE WISDOM OF UNDERSTANDING

Da Avabhasa's earliest Essays on the practice and Realization of "Radical" Understanding.

(These first two volumes of *The Knee of Listening,* taken from the original, unabridged manuscript and including recent commentary by Da Avabhasa and His devotees, are nearly twice the length of the previously published edition of *The Knee of Listening.*)
New Standard Edition (forthcoming, 1992)

VOLUME III

THE METHOD OF THE SIDDHAS: TALKS ON THE SPIRITUAL TECHNIQUE OF THE SAVIORS OF MANKIND

In this book of powerful and often extremely humorous Talks with devotees in 1972 and 1973, the first year of His formal Teaching Work, Da Avabhasa Reveals the Secret of the Way of Satsang—the profound and

transforming relationship between the Sat-Guru and His devotee.
New Standard Edition (forthcoming, 1992)

SCIENTIFIC PROOF OF THE EXISTENCE OF GOD WILL SOON BE ANNOUNCED BY THE WHITE HOUSE!
PROPHETIC WISDOM ABOUT THE MYTHS AND IDOLS OF MASS CULTURE AND POPULAR RELIGIOUS CULTISM, THE NEW PRIESTHOOD OF SCIENTIFIC AND POLITICAL MATERIALISM, AND THE SECRETS OF ENLIGHTENMENT HIDDEN IN THE BODY OF MAN

Speaking as a modern Prophet, Da Avabhasa combines His urgent critique of present-day society with a challenge to create true sacred community based on actual Divine Communion and a Spiritual and Transcendental Vision of human Destiny.
New Standard Edition (forthcoming, 1992)

THE TRANSMISSION OF DOUBT
TALKS AND ESSAYS ON THE TRANSCENDENCE OF SCIENTIFIC MATERIALISM THROUGH "RADICAL" UNDERSTANDING

Da Avabhasa's principal critique of scientific materialism, the dominant philosophy and world-view of modern humanity that suppresses our native impulse to Liberation, and His Revelation of the ancient and ever-new Way that is the true sacred science of Life, or of Divine Being Itself.
New Standard Edition (forthcoming, 1992)

THE ENLIGHTENMENT OF THE WHOLE BODY
A RATIONAL AND NEW PROPHETIC REVELATION OF THE TRUTH OF RELIGION, ESOTERIC SPIRITUALITY, AND THE DIVINE DESTINY OF MAN

One of Da Avabhasa's early Revelations of the Way of Eternal Life that He Offers to beings everywhere, including Ecstatic Confessions of His own Enlightened Realization of the Divine Person, and sublime Instruction in the practices of the Way of the Heart. When initially published in 1978, this text was a comprehensive summary of His Way of the Heart. Includes a unique section, with illustrations, on the esoteric anatomy of the advanced and the ultimate stages of Spiritual transformation.
New Standard Edition (forthcoming, 1992)

NIRVANASARA
Da Avabhasa critically appraises the sacred Wisdom-Culture of mankind, particularly focusing on the two most sublime traditions of sacred life and practice—Buddhism and Hindu non-dualism (Advaita Vedanta). Here He also announces and expounds upon His own Way of the Heart as the continuation and fulfillment of the most exalted Teachings of Buddhism and Hinduism.
New Standard Edition (forthcoming, 1992)

THE DREADED GOM-BOO, OR THE IMAGINARY DISEASE THAT RELIGION SEEKS TO CURE

In this remarkable book, Da Avabhasa Offers a startling and humorous insight: All religion seeks to cure us of an unreal or fundamentally imaginary disease, which He calls "the Dreaded Gom-Boo". This disease is our constant assumption that we have fallen from Grace and are thus in need of the salvatory "cure" of religious belief.

The good news of Da Avabhasa's Way of the Heart is that we need not seek to be cured but need only feel, observe, understand, and renounce (through the real ordeal of sacred practice) the very activity of seeking itself, and thus be restored to our native Happiness and Freedom.
New Standard Edition (forthcoming, 1992)

THE TEN FUNDAMENTAL QUESTIONS

Provocative Talks, Essays, and Leelas of Da Avabhasa, structured around the ten Great Questions that He has Given in His summary Source-Text, *The Dawn Horse Testament*. Through deeply "considering" these writings, we are drawn into direct feeling-intuition of both our inherent Divine Freedom and "what we are always doing" to become ego-bound. A powerful immersion in the Wisdom that inspires ordinary people to put God and Guru first in their lives by practicing the Way of the Heart.
(forthcoming, late 1991)

CRAZY DA MUST SING, INCLINED TO HIS WEAKER SIDE
CONFESSIONAL POEMS OF LIBERATION AND LOVE

Composed principally in the early 1970s and expressed spontaneously with the ardor of continuous, Divinely Awakened Identification with all beings, these remarkable poems proclaim Da Avabhasa's vulnerable human Love and His Mysterious, "Crazy" passion to Liberate others from ego-bondage.
$9.95 paper

THE SONG OF THE SELF SUPREME
ASHTAVAKRA GITA
The Classical Text of Atmadvaita by Ashtavakra

An authoritative translation of the *Ashtavakra Gita*, a text Da Avabhasa has described as "among the greatest (and most senior) communications of all the religious and Spiritual traditions of mankind". His illuminating Preface is a unique commentary on this grand classic of Advaita Vedanta, discussing the *Ashtavakra Gita* in the context of the total Great Tradition of Spiritual and Transcendental Wisdom. Da Avabhasa also identifies and discusses the characteristics of those rare texts and traditions that fully communicate the Realization and "Point of View" of the seventh, or fully Enlightened, stage of life.
New Standard Edition (forthcoming, 1992)

PRACTICAL TEXTS

THE EATING GORILLA COMES IN PEACE

THE TRANSCENDENTAL PRINCIPLE OF LIFE APPLIED TO DIET AND THE REGENERATIVE DISCIPLINE OF TRUE HEALTH

In a substantial reworking of the first edition of this text, Da Avabhasa Offers a practical manual of Divinely Inspired Wisdom about diet, health and healing, and the sacred approach to birthing and dying.

New Standard Edition (forthcoming, late 1991)

CONSCIOUS EXERCISE AND THE TRANSCENDENTAL SUN

THE PRINCIPLE OF LOVE APPLIED TO EXERCISE AND THE METHOD OF COMMON PHYSICAL ACTION. A SCIENCE OF WHOLE BODY WISDOM, OR TRUE EMOTION, INTENDED MOST ESPECIALLY FOR THOSE ENGAGED IN RELIGIOUS OR SPIRITUAL LIFE

Conscious exercise is a "technology of love"—which transforms physical exercise, play, and all ordinary activity into an embrace of the infinite energy of the cosmos, always in the conscious context of feeling-Contemplation of Da Avabhasa Himself as Divine Heart-Master. Greatly enlarged and updated from earlier editions.

New Standard Edition (forthcoming, mid-1991)

LOVE OF THE TWO-ARMED FORM

THE FREE AND REGENERATIVE FUNCTION OF SEXUALITY IN ORDINARY LIFE, AND THE TRANSCENDENCE OF SEXUALITY IN TRUE RELIGIOUS OR SPIRITUAL PRACTICE

Da Avabhasa's Instruction on the cultivation of "true intimacy" and the Realization of truly ecstatic, Spiritualized sexuality—a profound critique of both worldly exploitation of sex and ascetical, anti-sexual religious messages. As an alternative to these errors of West and East, Da Avabhasa proposes the specific practices of sexual "conscious exercise" and "sexual communion" (for individuals who practice in Satsang with Him). His Enlightened Wisdom-Teaching on sexuality Calls and inspires all men and women to a new and compassionate union of love, desire, and Spiritual consciousness.
New Standard Edition (forthcoming, 1992)

EASY DEATH

TALKS AND ESSAYS ON THE INHERENT AND ULTIMATE TRANSCENDENCE OF DEATH AND EVERYTHING ELSE

In this major revision of the popular first edition of His Talks and Essays on death, Da Avabhasa Reveals the esoteric secrets of the death process and Offers a wealth of practical Instruction on how to prepare for a God-Conscious and ecstatic transition from physical embodiment. Elisabeth Kübler-Ross wrote of *Easy Death:* "An exciting, stimulating, and thought-provoking book that adds immensely to the literature on the phenomena of life and death. Thank you for this masterpiece."
New Standard Edition (forthcoming, late 1991)

LEELAS

The Sanskrit term "leela" (sometimes "lila") traditionally refers to the Divine Play of the Sat-Guru with his (or her) devotees, whereby he Instructs and Liberates the world. Da Avabhasa has said that Leelas of His Instructional Play with His devotees are part of His own Word of Instruction, and they are, therefore, Potent with the Blessing and Awakening-Power of His Heart-Transmission.

THE CALLING OF THE KANYAS

CONFESSIONS OF SPIRITUAL AWAKENING AND "PERFECT PRACTICE" THROUGH THE LIBERATING GRACE OF THE DIVINE WORLD-TEACHER AND TRUE HEART-MASTER, DA AVABHASA (THE "BRIGHT")
by Meg McDonnell
with The Da Avabhasa Gurukula Kanyadana Kumari Order
(Kanya Tripura Rahasya, Kanya Samarpana Remembrance, Kanya Kaivalya Navaneeta, and Kanya Samatva Suprithi)

The story of the Graceful ordeal of sacred practice and transformation embraced by the formal renunciate order of four women devotees who personally serve Da Avabhasa. The confessions and the example of the Kanyas call everyone to deeply understand and heartily respond to the Supremely Blessed Event that has made their own Spiritual transformation possible: Da Avabhasa's Great Divine Emergence, beginning in early 1986 and continuing ever since. (forthcoming, 1992)

THE DIVINE EMERGENCE OF THE WORLD-TEACHER
THE REALIZATION, THE REVELATION, AND THE REVEALING ORDEAL OF DA KALKI
A Biographical Celebration of Heart-Master Da Love-Ananda
by Saniel Bonder

Never before have the Life and Work of a seventh stage Divine Incarnation been so carefully documented. This lively narrative focuses on Da Avabhasa's lifelong Ordeal of Divine Transmutation, which finally culminated, on January 11, 1986, in the Great Event that inaugurated His Divine Emergence as The World-Teacher and His ongoing Blessing Work.

Richly illustrated with more than 100 photographs of Da Avabhasa and full of the often dramatic Stories of His Teaching years and His Divine Emergence Work, as well as His own unique Confessions of Divine Incarnation, Realization, and Service to all beings. [The next edition of *The Divine Emergence of The World-Teacher* will be subtitled *The Realization, the Revelation, and the Revealing Ordeal of Da Avabhasa (The "Bright")*].
$14.95 paper

FOR AND ABOUT CHILDREN

WHAT AND WHERE AND WHO TO REMEMBER TO BE HAPPY
A SIMPLE EXPLANATION OF THE WAY OF THE HEART (FOR CHILDREN, AND EVERYONE ELSE)

A new edition of Da Avabhasa's essential Teaching-Revelation on the religious principles and practices appropriate for children. In Words easily understood and enjoyed by children and adults, Da Avabhasa tells children (and adults) how to "feel and breathe and Behold and Be the Mystery".
New Standard Edition, fully illustrated (forthcoming, 1992)

THE TWO SECRETS
(yours, AND MINE)

*A STORY OF HOW
THE WORLD-TEACHER, DA KALKI,
GAVE GREAT WISDOM AND BLESSING
HELP TO YOUNG PEOPLE (AND EVEN
OLDER PEOPLE, TOO) ABOUT
HOW TO REMEMBER WHAT AND
WHERE AND WHO TO REMEMBER TO
BE HAPPY*
*A Gift (Forever) from Da Kalki
(The World-Teacher, Heart-Master
Da Love-Ananda), as told by
Kanya Remembrance, Brahmacharini
Shawnee Free Jones, and their friends*

A moving account of a young girl's confrontation with the real demands of sacred practice, and how Da Avabhasa lovingly Instructed and Served her in her transition through a crisis of commitment to practice that every devotee must, at some point, endure.
$12.95 paper

VEGETABLE SURRENDER,

OR HAPPINESS IS NOT BLUE
by Heart-Master Da and two little girls

The humorous tale of Onion One-Yin and his vegetable friends, who embark on a search for someone who can teach them about happiness and love, and end up learning a great lesson about seeking. Beautifully illustrated with original line drawings.
$12.95 cloth, oversize

THE TRANSCENDENCE
OF CHILDHOOD
AND ADOLESCENCE

Compiled from Da Avabhasa's previously unpublished Instructions, this book comprehensively addresses the conscious education of young people in their teenage years, providing for the modern age an Enlightened vision of the ancient principle and way of life called "brahmacharya". In this approach, as practiced in the communities of Free Daists, young people (typically between the ages of 11 and 15) make a free and conscious choice to devote their lives to the Realization of the Divine Reality, under the direct tutelage of their "brahmacharya master" or Guru. This book presents a "radical" vision of education that is virtually unknown in the modern West.
(forthcoming, 1992)

LOOK AT THE SUNLIGHT ON
THE WATER

*EDUCATING CHILDREN FOR A LIFE OF
SELF-TRANSCENDING LOVE AND
HAPPINESS: AN INTRODUCTION*

Full of eminently practical guidance for the "whole bodily" and sacred education of children and young people, this simple, straightforward, informative text is also perhaps the best available brief summation of Da Avabhasa's Wisdom on the first three stages of life, or the period from infancy to adulthood.
$12.95 paper

PERIODICALS

THE FREE DAIST

The Bi-Monthly Journal of the Heart-Word and Blessing Work of The Divine World-Teacher and True Heart-Master, Da Avabhasa

The Free Daist chronicles the Leelas of the Teaching Work and the Divine Emergence Work of Da Avabhasa, and describes the practice and process of devotion, self-discipline, self-understanding, service, and meditation in the Way of the Heart. In addition, the magazine reports on the cultural and missionary activities of The Free Daist Communion and the cooperative community of Da Avabhasa's devotees. Of special interest is the regular "Hermitage Chronicle" offering current news of Da Avabhasa's Life and Work.

Subscriptions are US$48.00 per year for six issues. Please send your check or money order (payable to The Dawn Horse Press) to:
The Free Daist, P.O. Box 3680, Clearlake, CA 95422, USA

THE "BRIGHT"

Celebrations of The Divine World-Teacher, Da Avabhasa (The "Bright")

A brief bi-monthly periodical, oriented to the general reader, introducing the Good News of Da Avabhasa and His Work and countering the trends of scientific materialism, religious provincialism, and anti-guruism in present-day society.

Subscriptions are US$12.00 per year for six issues. Please send your check or money order (payable to The Dawn Horse Press) to:
The "Bright", P.O. Box 3680, Clearlake, CA 95422, USA

A subscription to *The "Bright"* is complimentary with each subscription to *The Free Daist*.

AUDIO-VISUAL PUBLICATIONS

THE WAY OF THE HEART

ON THE "RADICAL" SPIRITUAL TEACHING
AND UNIVERSAL BLESSING WORK OF
THE WESTERN-BORN ADEPT

HEART-MASTER
DA LOVE-ANANDA

VIDEOTAPES

THE WAY OF THE HEART

An Introduction to the "Radical" Teaching and Blessing Work of the Western-Born Adept, Da Avabhasa (The Divine World-Teacher and True Heart-Master, Da Love-Ananda Hridayam)

Incorporating rare segments of recent and historical footage, Part One tells the Story of Sri Da Avabhasa's Illumined Birth and His Ordeal of Divine Re-Awakening for others, and celebrates the Emergence of His Work of World Blessing. Part Two (which includes Talk excerpts by Da Avabhasa and testimonials by long-time practitioners) describes the Gifts and forms of practice that are Given to all who take up the Way of the Heart as Da Avabhasa's devotees. Part Three introduces the sacred culture of the Way of the Heart.
$29.95, 2 hours, VHS, NTSC or PAL format

The Way of the Heart is also available in a modified form, which includes recent footage of Da Avabhasa in Darshan with devotees and other material not included in the full-length version. A brief, summary audio-visual introduction to His Life and Divine Work as the World-Teacher in a world addicted to egoic suffering and seeking. $19.95, 76 minutes, VHS, NTSC or PAL format

ORDERING THE BOOKS AND VIDEOTAPES OF DA AVABHASA

The books and videotapes of Da Avabhasa are available at local bookstores and by mail from The Dawn Horse Book Depot.

Please write to us at the address below for a complete catalogue of books, study courses, and audio-visual publications on the Way of the Heart and traditional sacred literature.

In the USA please add $1.75 for the first book or videotape and $.75 for each additional book or videotape. California residents add 6% sales tax.

Outside the USA please add $4.00 for the first book or videotape and $1.00 for each additional book or videotape.

To order the books and videotapes listed above, and to receive your copy of The Dawn Horse Book Depot Catalogue, please write:

The Dawn Horse Book Depot
P.O. Box 3680
Clearlake, CA 95422, USA
(707) 928-4936

An Invitation to Responsibility

The Way of the Heart that Sri Da Avabhasa has Revealed is an invitation to everyone to assume real responsibility for his or her life. As Sri Da Avabhasa has Said in *The Dawn Horse Testament,* "If any one Is Interested In The Realization Of The Heart, Let him or her First Submit (Formally, and By Heart) To Me, and (Thereby) Commence The Ordeal Of self-Observation, self-Understanding, and self-Transcendence." Therefore, participation in the Way of the Heart requires a real struggle with oneself, and not at all a struggle with Sri Da Avabhasa, or with others.

All who study the Way of the Heart or take up its practice should remember that they are responding to a Call to become responsible for themselves. They should understand that they, not Sri Da Avabhasa or others, are responsible for any decision they may make or action they take in the course of their lives of study or practice. This has always been true, and it is true whatever the individual's involvement in the Way of the Heart, be it as one who studies Da Avabhasa's Wisdom-Teaching, or as a formal Friend of The Free Daist Communion, or as a participant in Da Avabhasa International, or as a formally acknowledged member of The Free Daist Communion.

Honoring and Protecting the Sacred Word through Perpetual Copyright

Since ancient times, practitioners of true religion and Spirituality have valued, above all, time spent in the Company of the Sat-Guru, or one who has Realized God, Truth, or Reality, and who Serves that same Realization in others. Such practitioners understand that the Sat-Guru literally Transmits his or her (Realized) State to every one (and every thing) with which he or she comes in contact. Through this Transmission, objects, environments, and rightly prepared individuals with which the Sat-Guru has contact can become Empowered, or Imbued with the Sat-Guru's Transforming Power. It is by this process of Empowerment that things and beings are made truly and literally sacred, and things so sanctified thereafter function as a Source of the Sat-Guru's Blessing for all who understand how to make right and sacred use of them.

The Sat-Guru and all that he Empowers are, therefore, truly Sacred Treasures, for they help draw the practitioner more quickly into the Realization of Perfect Identity with the Divine Self. Cultures of true Wisdom have always understood that such Sacred Treasures are precious (and fragile) Gifts to humanity, and that they should be honored, protected, and reserved for right sacred use. Indeed, the word "sacred" means "set apart", and thus protected, from the secular world. Sri Da Avabhasa is a Sat-Guru of the Most Perfect degree. He has Conformed His body-mind completely to the Divine Self, and He is thus a most Potent Source of Blessing-Transmission of God, Truth, or Reality. He has for many years Empowered, or made sacred, special places and things, and these now Serve as His Divine Agents, or as literal expressions and extensions of His Blessing-Transmission. Among these Empowered Sacred Treasures is His Wisdom-Teaching, which is Full of His Transforming Power. This Blessed and Blessing Wisdom-Teaching has Mantric Force, or the literal Power to Serve God-Realization in those who are Graced to receive it.

Therefore, Sri Da Avabhasa's Wisdom-Teaching must be perpetually honored and protected, "set apart" from all possible interference and wrong use. The Free Daist Communion, which is the fellowship of devotees of Sri Da Avabhasa, is committed to the perpetual preservation and right honoring of the sacred Wisdom-Teaching of the Way of the Heart. But it is also true that in order to fully accomplish this we must find support in the world-society in which we live and from the laws under which we live. Thus, we call for a world-society and for laws that acknowledge the Sacred, and that permanently protect It from insensitive, secular interference and wrong use of any kind. We call for, among other things, a system of law that acknowledges that the Wisdom-Teaching of the Way of the Heart, in all Its forms, is, because of Its sacred nature, protected by perpetual copyright.

We invite others who respect the Sacred to join with us in this call and in working toward its realization. And, even in the meantime, we claim that all copyrights to the Wisdom-Teaching of Sri Da Avabhasa and the other sacred literature and recordings of the Way of the Heart are of perpetual duration.

We make this claim on behalf of Sri Love-Anandashram (Naitauba) Pty Ltd, which, acting as trustee of the Sri Love-Anandashram (Naitauba) Trust, is the holder of all such copyrights.

Da Avabhasa and the Sacred Treasures of Free Daism

Those who Realize God bring great Blessing and Divine Possibility for the world. As Free Adepts, they Accomplish universal Blessing Work that benefits everything and everyone. Such Realizers also Work very specifically and intentionally with individuals who approach them as their devotees, and with those places where they reside, and to which they Direct their specific Regard for the sake of perpetual Spiritual Empowerment. This was understood in traditional Spiritual cultures, and those cultures therefore found ways to honor Realizers, to provide circumstances for them where they were free to do their Divine Work without obstruction or interference.

Those who value Sri Da Avabhasa's Realization and Service have always endeavored to appropriately honor Him in this traditional way, to provide a circumstance where He is completely Free to Do His

Divine Work. Since 1983, Sri Da Avabhasa has resided principally on the Island of Naitauba, Fiji, also known as Sri Love-Anandashram. This island has been set aside by Free Daists worldwide as a Place for Sri Da Avabhasa to Do His universal Blessing Work for the sake of everyone and His specific Work with those who pilgrimage to Sri Love-Anandashram to receive the special Blessing of coming into His physical Company.

Sri Da Avabhasa is a legal renunciate. He owns nothing and He has no secular or religious institutional function. He Functions only in Freedom. He, and the other members of The Naitauba (Free Daist) Order of Sannyasins, the senior renunciate order of Free Daism, are provided for by the Sri Love-Anandashram (Naitauba) Trust, which also provides for Sri Love-Anandashram altogether and ensures the permanent integrity of Sri Da Avabhasa's Wisdom-Teaching, both in its archival and in its published forms. This Trust, which functions only in Fiji, exists exclusively to provide for these Sacred Treasures of Free Daism.

Outside Fiji, the institution which has developed in response to Sri Da Avabhasa's Wisdom-Teaching and universal Blessing is known as The Free Daist Communion. The Free Daist Communion is active worldwide in making Da Avabhasa's Wisdom-Teaching available to all, in offering guidance to all who are moved to respond to His Offering, and in providing for the other Sacred Treasures of Free Daism, including The Mountain Of Attention Sanctuary (in California) and Tumomama Sanctuary (in Hawaii). In addition to the central corporate entity of The Free Daist Communion, which is based in California, there are numerous regional entities which serve congregations of Sri Da Avabhasa's devotees in various places throughout the world.

Free Daists worldwide have also established numerous community organizations, through which they provide for many of their common and cooperative community needs, including needs relating to housing, food, businesses, medical care, schools, and death and dying. By attending to these and all other ordinary human concerns and affairs via self-transcending cooperation and mutual effort, Sri Da Avabhasa's devotees constantly free their energy and attention, both personally and collectively, for practice of the Way of the Heart and for service to Sri Da Avabhasa, to Sri Love-Anandashram, to the other Sacred Treasures of Free Daism, and to The Free Daist Communion.

All of the organizations that have evolved in response to Sri Da Avabhasa and His Offering are legally separate from one another, and each has its own purpose and function. He neither directs, nor bears responsibility for, the activities of these organizations. Again, He Functions only in Freedom. These organizations represent the collective intention of Free Daists worldwide not only to provide for the Sacred Treasures of Free Daism, but also to make Da Avabhasa's Offering of the Way of the Heart universally available to all.

AN INVITATION

Of all the means for Spiritual growth and ultimate Liberation offered in the sacred traditions of humankind, the most treasured is the Way of Satsang, or the Way lived in the Blessing Company of One Who has Realized the Truth. Da Avabhasa, The Divine World-Teacher and True Heart-Master, Da Love-Ananda Hridayam, Offers just such a rare and Graceful Opportunity.

The transformative relationship to Da Avabhasa is the foundation of the Way of the Heart that He Offers. Through a whole personal and collective life of self-transcending practice in His Company, ordinary men and women may be purified of their egoic suffering and enjoy the Blessings of a God-Realizing destiny.

If you would like to receive a free introductory brochure or talk to a practicing devotee about forms of participation in the Way of the Heart, please write or call our Correspondence Department:

Correspondence Department
The Free Daist Communion
P.O. Box 3680
Clearlake, California 95422 USA

(707) 928-4936